BLOOMSBURY
A SQUARE MILE

Bedford Square

BLOOMSBURY
A SQUARE MILE

A History and Guide

By Edward Arnold

Grosvenor House
Publishing Limited

This book is published by
Grosvenor House Publishing Ltd
Link House
140 The Broadway, Tolworth, Surrey, KT6 7HT.
www.grosvenorhousepublishing.co.uk

A CIP record for this book
is available from the British Library

ISBN 978-1-78623-445-2

To my wonderful wife Lynn, for her loving support together with endless supplies of coffee.

ACKNOWLEDGEMENTS

This book could not have materialised without the contributions from so many people, institutions, businesses and organisations that shared their knowledge and wisdom with me. The phrase 'if you don't ask...' certainly comes to mind because when I asked, I was flooded with answers. I received advice, guidance and information from many busy people from businesses, local residents to academics at both the UL and UCL. Both universities gave me privileged access during my visits and despite their demanding schedules, found the time to give me expert advice and valuable contributions.

I would especially like the following contributors to know just how grateful I am: Anthony Walker-Cook, doctoral candidate in the Department of English Studies at UCL, freelance editor and theatre critic. Thank you for methodically and enthusiastically checking historical detail and supplying some very useful additional research.

Dr Juliette Atkinson (UCL English) for her encouragement and assistance.

Taylor Boxall, Media Commercial Affairs and Acquisitions Manager, lecturer and entrepreneur whose advice, extraordinary support, friendship and energetic feedback kept me going to the bitter end.

My appreciation also goes to Sandra Elliott, UL, for her determination in obtaining historical information and images of Senate House. Olwen Myhill, UL, for supplying historical maps and advice.

David Smith and David Plumb, Lazari Investments Limited, for their in-depth information about The Brunswick. James Doyle, Souvenir Press Ltd, for investigating historical information about the company. Holly Peel, Wellcome Collection, for selecting some perfect images. Ed Nassau Lake, Jarndyce Antiquarian Booksellers, for their beautiful shop interior photograph and encouragement.

FOREWORD

In all the years that I've known Ed, I've always been able to rely on his infinite capacity to conjure up stories from his past. His travels around the world, his eclectic mix of life experiences and his propensity for often being in the right place at the right time or, as he might have you believe, the wrong place at the wrong time, have all provided a great many hours of incredulity and marvel.

So, when he told me that he was writing a book not only was I not in the least surprised, I was proud that he would choose his new project to be such a personal one. Having first met in the pseudo-calm of an arts and humanities teacher's office in a college in the heart of England, his passion for the education and development of his students was second to none. I would often find Ed turning up early to get materials prepped or buzzing around the office in his spare time to help out a flustered A-level student. To have been part of this journey and to have earned enough of his respect that he should ask me for opinions, feedback and an objective, critical eye is a privilege.

The book that you hold in your hands has opened my eyes to all manner of fascinating moments in history and secret areas to explore. Armed with the knowledge the following pages provide, I walk through Bloomsbury with an entirely new perspective and appreciation of the area. Street names suddenly mean so much more, building façades now hold significance far beyond the superficial, and the gardens and backstreets have suddenly taken on a whole new meaning. I take guests to Malet Street Gardens to enjoy some respite from the bustle of Tottenham Court Road and Oxford Street, I sip a coffee at Bloomsbury Coffee House and often I'll just wander the streets to gaze up at the architecture and imagine life here one hundred years ago.

If you've picked up this book out of curiosity, I'd recommend going one step further and reading it. This is not a dusty, old history book about a few streets and some forgettable architecture, it's a zippy read about some remarkable people and places tucked away in a city full of both...

Taylor Boxall – friend, Manager, Commercial Affairs and Acquisitions (Media), lecturer, entrepreneur. London.

INTRODUCTION

One is spoilt for choice when it comes to choosing a history or guidebook about London. Wander into any bookstore and there'll be shelves of books for all manner of types: wartime London, where to eat, where to take a walk, why the Thames is so dirty, street guides and local guides. Some people pick out comprehensive guides to fully understand every aspect of the city and some opt for a concise pocket guide read.

I offer you something in-between: an all-in-one straightforward history and present-day guide of the Bloomsbury area, drawing your attention to places of interest and the histories associated with them within bite-sized sections. Short stories and facts unfold revealing fascinating glimpses into the buildings and former inhabitants. In this book, I unite the past with the present, aided by the images and maps that illustrate the many places waiting to be (re)discovered and explored. Photographs highlight the contrasting variety of areas that lie within this district and I reveal how this complex neighbourhood achieved such an influential presence. You will gain a solid foundation of knowledge that will allow you more time to enjoy and appreciate this captivating area.

CONTENTS

Bloomsbury (bluːmzb(ə)ri), n. The vibrant, intellectual and cultural heart of London, located within the southern part of the London Borough of Camden; renowned for its Georgian streets, garden squares, writers, artists and thinkers; home to universities, medical institutions, The British Museum and independent bookshops.

WHY WRITE ABOUT BLOOMSBURY, AND WHY NOW?

The journey to writing this book began as a tale of self-discovery. My mother was an Irish immigrant who arrived in Bloomsbury in the mid-1950s with little more than hand luggage to her name and a will for a new and better life. Between 1956 and 1977, both my mother and her aunt worked as residential maids at the once neatly named Cranston's Ivanhoe Hotel, now less neatly named The Radisson Blu Edwardian Bloomsbury Street Hotel in Bloomsbury Street. The hotel was, for a long period, their home. My Italian father was a chef at the nearby Warwick Hotel that is now The Cheshire Hotel in Great Russell Street.

I was born at the University College Hospital in 1964 and baptised at The Church of St Anselm and St Cæcilia on the east side of Kingsway, near Holborn Station. The early part of my life started at 27 Montague Street, now The Museum Hostel, directly opposite the east side of The British Museum. Originally built in the nineteenth century for the well-off middle classes, during the 1960s this house accommodated not so well-off, hotel domestic staff. Mothers had to battle up two flights of stairs before arriving at their cramped and basic living quarters. With little government support in those days, being a single mother on a minimum wage and despite her best efforts my mother, sadly, could no longer support me. She did the single most selfless thing a mother could do, and by 1970 I was fostered and eventually adopted.

I was adopted by the most caring and loving parents a child could ever wish for and grew up outside of London. I grew up with a thirst for exploration and once I was old enough my inquisitive nature took me further and further afield. Throughout my twenties I travelled the world before I met the love of my life, Lynn. In typically adventurous style, we went backpacking together and got married on Easter Island, Chile in 1993. Soon after settling into a blissful married life, I returned to university and studied to become a media lecturer.

Some years ago, I decided to go on a personal quest to reconnect with my past: a past that, for many years, I had often thought about. Boarding a train one unusually mild January morning and disembarking at St Pancras, I realised that Bloomsbury, this tiny fraction of one of the world's greatest cities, was special, but it would be some time later before I truly understood why.

Despite my numerous stays over the years I am as fascinated by Bloomsbury as ever and have come to rely on the fact that it never ceases to surprise and inspire me. So, for that reason, I would like to share with you this very special part of London. My aim is to turn a place that you have heard of into a friend that you will want to visit.

A BRIEF DESCRIPTION OF BLOOMSBURY

Bloomsbury, the intellectual and literary heart of the city, is a microcosm of everything great about London. The entire area fits comfortably within a square mile, making it one of central London's easiest and safest places to get around on foot. Filled with charming architectural rows of Georgian terraces, and places such as the still futuristic Brunswick building and the world famous British Museum, Bloomsbury is a dense and unintimidating place to visit; every corner you turn, every building you see, has a place in history and has many stories to tell. This book will reveal some of London's finest square gardens and green spaces that echo with the poetry and literature of the Bloomsbury Group and great writers such as Charles Dickens. One will discover two great historic universities that led the way in equality and diversity before the term was even fully understood!

Bloomsbury, a centre of science and research, is littered with an array of medical schools and institutions together with the pioneering Great Ormond Street Hospital and the ultra-modern University College London Hospital. One will learn about the abundance of social reformers such as Captain Thomas Coram, who established The Foundling Hospital, and the humanistic approach adopted throughout the district that prevails today and is evident in the progressive character of the place. This square mile of learning and creativity has had an important influence on the world, yet despite this, there is no snobbery here, the area has a down-to-earth laid back, happy atmosphere. Here one will find a youthful and diverse mix of people who study, work and live within the area. With such a lot to boast about, this unpretentious slice of unspoilt London modestly continues its daily life. So, to discover what a poet and a lawyer can achieve in Bloomsbury and why the corpse of one of the most important philosophers in modern history is kept on display in a university hallway, where to buy medieval Norman jewellery or learn about Bloomsbury's presence in the world, read on and enjoy.

Bloomsbury Festival, 2018

WHERE IS BLOOMSBURY?

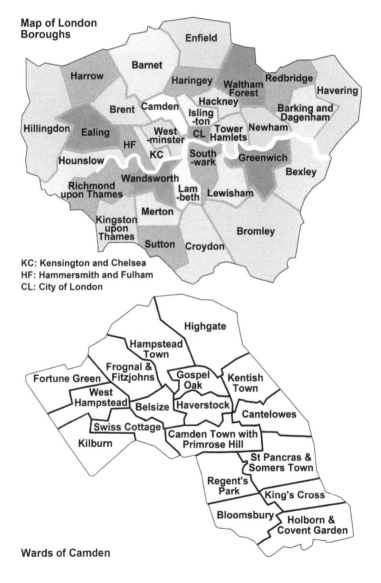

Map of London Boroughs

Enfield

Barnet

Harrow

Haringey

Waltham Forest

Redbridge

Havering

Brent

Camden

Hackney

Isling-ton

Barking and Dagenham

Hillingdon

Ealing

West-minster

CL

Tower Hamlets

Newham

HF

KC

South-wark

Greenwich

Bexley

Hounslow

Wandsworth

Richmond upon Thames

Lam-beth

Lewisham

Merton

Kingston upon Thames

Sutton

Croydon

Bromley

KC: Kensington and Chelsea
HF: Hammersmith and Fulham
CL: City of London

Highgate

Hampstead Town

Frognal & Fitzjohns

Gospel Oak

Kentish Town

Fortune Green

West Hampstead

Belsize

Haverstock

Cantelowes

Swiss Cottage

Kilburn

Camden Town with Primrose Hill

St Pancras & Somers Town

Regent's Park

King's Cross

Bloomsbury

Holborn & Covent Garden

Wards of Camden

5

Bloomsbury is an area with boundaries that are a little difficult to define and have always been under dispute; therefore, no officially recognised boundary exists. Situated in the southern part of the London Borough of Camden, the electoral ward of Bloomsbury is relatively small compared to what many Londoners regard as Bloomsbury.

For the purposes of this book, I will draw my own boundaries, and those start in the north at one of London's busiest roads: Euston Road, where King's Cross, St Pancras and Euston railway stations feed the capital with an endless supply of commuters and travellers. I also include the ward of King's Cross, using Gray's Inn Road as the eastern edge for my unofficial map. I steal a small part of Holborn and Covent Garden to the south and to complete my area to the west, I will borrow a small piece of Fitzrovia as far as Charlotte Street and Fitzroy Square.

The map above shows the area covered in this book with red lines depicting Camden ward boundaries. Please note that Fitzrovia is a neighbourhood that lies (in part) within the ward of Bloomsbury.

A BRIEF HISTORY

Bloomsbury

The earliest record of the Bloomsbury area was in the 1086 *Domesday Book* that was commissioned by William the Conqueror. The book described the area as being 'of vineyards and wood for at least 100 pigs'. The name Bloomsbury originates from Blemondisberi, when in 1201 Norman landowner William de Blemond acquired the land (believed to be around today's Bloomsbury Square). The word 'bury' derives from the Anglo-Saxon 'burh', meaning a fort or fortified place, hamlet or seat, hence the 'bury' or manor, of Blemond. King Edward III acquired Blemond's land, which was in turn handed to the Carthusian monks of the London Charterhouse at the end of the fourteenth century. The land in this area continued to be mainly rural.

The sixteenth century, saw the Dissolution of the Monasteries (1536–40). Henry VIII took the monastery and land back and granted it to Thomas Wriothesley, 1st Earl of Southampton in 1545. From the mid-seventeenth century, Wriothesley's great-grandson started to develop the Bloomsbury area. In 1667, Lady Rachel Vaughan inherited the estate and married William, Lord Russell in 1669, bringing the estate into the Russell family. William was beheaded for treason in 1683. Lady Rachel ran the Bloomsbury Estate until her death in 1723 when the estate was taken over by the Bedford Estate.

By 1753, The British Museum was founded thanks to the collections of physician Sir Hans Sloane who bequeathed his entire collection, as a gift to the nation. From 1775 to 1783, the development of Bedford Square transformed the pastures of northern Bloomsbury into an upper-middle-class restricted district.

London University was founded in 1826 and in 1834 North London Hospital was built in Gower Street providing the university with a medical school.

The London and Birmingham Railway built Euston Station which opened in 1837 and within a year had become London's first intercity railway. The London hub of the Great Northern Railway, King's Cross Station, first opened as a temporary passenger station in 1850 and was located in the Midland Goods Shed. The current station was opened in 1852 to the designs of architect Lewis Cubitt. Architects George Gilbert Scott and William Henry Barlow's St Pancras Station opened in 1868.

By the mid-1800s Bloomsbury, and the later named Fitzrovia, had started to gain a reputation as a literary and cultural hotspot. In 1851, Charles Dickens took out a lease on Tavistock House in Tavistock Square. A group of intellectuals that included English writers, philosophers, and artists started to descend upon the Bloomsbury area from around 1904 until the early 1930s. These famous intellects became known as the Bloomsbury Group.

In 1937, the University of London opened their new towering headquarters, Senate House.

Bloomsbury received a considerable amount of damage throughout the London Blitz of 1940–41. The 1950s saw Bloomsbury slowly heal with the rest of the country. By the 1960s and 1970s, the area saw new modernist developments such as the iconic Centre Point building and The Brunswick. In 1997, The British Museum's library moved to new purpose-built premises in Euston Road under the new name of The British Library and officially opened in 1998.

Fitzrovia

The area now known as Fitzrovia is associated with Tottenhall Manor and is mentioned in the *Domesday Book* as being owned by the Dean and Chapter of Saint Paul's Cathedral until 1560. *John Rocque's map of London, 1746* shows that the manor house itself was roughly located at the north end of present-day Tottenham Court Road, where Euston Road underpass lies. Euston Road was originally called The New Road and was built in 1756 as a means of moving livestock.

Charles Fitzroy, lord of the manor of Tottenhall, began development of the Bloomsbury part of the Fitzroy Estate during the late eighteenth century. Fitzroy Square was intended for the upper classes; however, by the end of the eighteenth century, Belgravia and Mayfair were becoming very fashionable places to live. This drew the upper classes away from Fitzrovia, leaving houses open to subdivision into smaller accommodation and workshops for let. At this time, the area received many immigrants from France and neighbouring countries, and gained a reputation as a centre for the furniture trade with artisans such as Thomas Chippendale moving to London and living close by in Covent Garden.

During the 1800s, many residential buildings were repurposed for non-residential usage. Some houses were converted into hotels to serve the new railway terminals along Euston Road. From the mid-1800s to the early 1900s cheaper housing was available, attracting bohemians to the area including the author Virginia Woolf (see chapter on the Bloomsbury Group).

Fitzrovia, by the early 1900s, was increasing in population with streets such as Cleveland Street, Whitfield Street, Maple Street and Warren Street flourishing with successful shops and businesses. A public house called the Fitzroy Tavern became a popular watering hole for many intellectuals and bohemians, and it is widely accepted that Fitzrovia got its name from this fine establishment in around 1940. After the Second World War Italians, Greeks, Nepalese and Bengalis came to Fitzrovia. By now, there was a demand for commercial space and Fitzrovia lost some of its fine Georgian buildings.

In 1994, Fitzrovia appeared on the Ordnance Survey maps. Property developers attempted to rename the area Noho – meaning north of Soho; an attempt which was fortunately vetoed and never came to pass. Today, Fitzrovia is a cosmopolitan, vibrant and trendy mix of interesting shops, businesses, pubs and restaurants with a media and advertising presence. Fitzrovia has a strong community spirit and a proud neighbourhood association.

Thomas Wriothesley, First Earl of Southampton – Artist: Hans Holbein the Younger

THE BLOOMSBURY GROUP

'Lived in squares, painted in circles and loved in triangles'

American writer Dorothy Parker's famous witticism about
the Bloomsbury Group.

Roger Fry: Still Life with Omega Flowers, 1919

Like other subjects I have touched upon in this book, the Bloomsbury Group is indeed a book within itself. I will simply introduce this important milestone in world literacy and culture in the hope that you will pursue further research and reading. This modest introduction to the Bloomsbury Group is told through the life of Virginia Woolf.

The epicentre of this earthquake in art, culture and thinking started in Gordon Square where a circle of intellectuals, writers and artists began to meet up from around 1904, eventually sending cultural aftershocks around the world. They were mostly privileged and well-educated individuals, who rejected the old Victorian ideals and discussed, questioned and challenged art, sexuality, politics, literature and philosophy. These friends often lived and worked together and expressed their ideas through their own genres. By the 1930s, the group began to decline due to the deaths of several members and changing social attitudes. Today the Bloomsbury Group are regarded as a milestone in British art, literature and social progress.

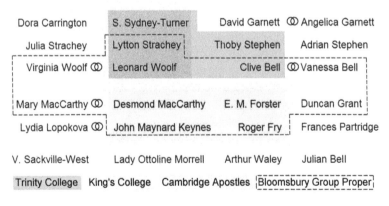

Some of the members of the Bloomsbury Group

The key members of the Bloomsbury Group were:

Clive Bell (1881–1964), art critic who helped popularise Post-Impressionism in Great Britain.

In 1907, he married Vanessa Stephen, (sister of Virginia Woolf). The marriage became open and ultimately unsuccessful but they never officially separated or divorced and remained friends. In 1914, Bell devised significant form theory that promoted the idea that the form of an artwork or forms within it can be expressive, even if it is non-realistic and unrecognisable.

'lines and colours combined in a particular way, certain forms, and relations of forms, stir our aesthetic emotions'.

Clive Bell: *Art* (1914)

Vanessa Bell (1879–1961), née Stephen. Post-Impressionist painter and designer.

Clive Bell and Vanessa were the founding members of the Bloomsbury Group.

Often overlooked, this talented artist's early work was considered pleasant and conventional. In 1910, Bell became inspired by the works of Matisse, Cézanne and Picasso when she visited England's first Post-Impressionist exhibition. After the exhibition she wrote, 'here was a sudden pointing to a possible path, a sudden liberation and encouragement to feel for oneself which were absolutely overwhelming.' Bell took her vibrant modernist style to the Omega Workshops in 1913, expressing her ideas in the many products they produced.

Roger Fry (1866–1934), art critic and Post-Impressionist painter, founder of the Omega Workshops and regarded as the champion of the movement, he termed, Post-Impressionism. He was known for his rich, straightforward and naturalistic paintings.

In 1913, Fry opened Omega Workshops Ltd at 33 Fitzroy Square in Fitzrovia. The premises had studios where products were designed by artists anonymously. Fry's belief was that objects should be desired for their beauty rather than the artist's reputation.

Items for sale in the showrooms ranged from household accessories to furniture and fabrics all under the Omega designs symbol: Ω. The directors were Roger Fry, Vanessa Bell and Duncan Grant, all of whom had formed a deep friendship through the Bloomsbury Group.

The Omega Workshops led the way for contemporary art and design often incorporating Post-Impressionist and Cubist styles. Sadly, due to financial difficulties the workshops only lasted six years and closed in 1919 but left a lasting impression in the world of art and design.

Duncan Grant (1885–1978), Post-Impressionist painter and designer.

Grant was amongst the first English artists to assimilate the Post-Impressionists style of Paul Cézanne and the bright, bold and daring styles of the French Fauvist group.

Despite being homosexual, Grant formed a close relationship with Vanessa Bell who was married to Clive Bell. In 1918, she became pregnant giving Grant a daughter Angelica, whom Clive Bell raised as his own daughter. Duncan and Vanessa lived together in a platonic and open relationship for most of their lives, often working together and sharing creative ideas.

E. M. Forster (1879–1970), novelist, essayist, social and literary critic.

Edward Morgan Forster is known for his novels such as *Howards End* (1910) and *A Passage to India* (1924), short stories and his critical observations and support of liberal humanism. By the 1930s and 1940s he became a celebrated broadcaster on BBC Radio and was associated with the Union of Ethical Societies. He wrote articles that opposed censorship and was an advocate of individual liberty.

'If I had to choose between betraying my country and betraying my friend, I hope I should have the guts to betray my country.'

E. M. Forster: *Two Cheers for Democracy* (1951)

John Maynard Keynes (1883–1946), economist, journalist, and financier.

Keynes was best known for Keynesian economics: the causes of prolonged unemployment. His last major work, that proved to be one of the most influential economics books ever written: *The General Theory of Employment, Interest and Money* (1936), gave theoretical support to the idea that full employment, sponsored by government would help solve economic recession.

'The long run is a misleading guide to current affairs. In the long run we are all dead.'

John Maynard Keynes: *A Tract on Monetary Reform* (1923)

'If you owe your bank a hundred pounds, you have a problem. But if you owe a million, it has.'

John Maynard Keynes: as quoted in *The Economist* (1982)

Desmond MacCarthy (1877–1952), literary journalist.

MacCarthy was known and respected for his great knowledge, sensitive judgment and literary merit. His career started as a freelance journalist and by 1913 he became a drama critic for the *New Statesman*. By 1928, he was also senior literary critic to *The Sunday Times*. MacCarthy was keen to promote undiscovered new authors. His own work included: *Portraits* (1931), *Drama* (1940), and *Shaw* (1951). MacCarthy's contributions and good work were rewarded when he was knighted in 1951.

Lytton Strachey (1880–1932), biographer and critic.

He was loved and hated for his wit and ironic prose style. He had little respect for the past and preferred to 'get to the point', making him a predominant figure of literary modernism. Strachey is best known for *Eminent Victorians* (1918) – a collection of short biographical sketches. This collection of sketches portrayed Victorian heroes Cardinal Manning, Florence Nightingale, Thomas Arnold, and General Charles 'Chinese' Gordon with irreverence and wit.

Leonard Woolf (1880–1969), essayist and author, political theorist, publisher, social reformer, co-founder of the Hogarth Press in 1917.

As a young man in 1904, Woolf moved to Ceylon (now Sri Lanka) and served in the Ceylon Civil Service returning to England in 1911. The following year he married Virginia Stephen. Leonard Woolf was a man admired for his moral fibre, as reflected in his autobiography that was written in volumes over the course of his life. The volumes are: *Sowing* (1960), *Growing* (1961), *Beginning Again* (1964), *Downhill All the Way* (1967), and *The Journey Not the Arrival Matters* (1969). Woolf had some political influence and his left wing editorial activity helped to pave the way for the policies of the League of Nations, the United Nations and the welfare state.

'Anyone can be a barbarian; it requires a terrible effort to remain a civilized man.'

Leonard Woolf: *Barbarians Within and Without* (1939)

Virginia Woolf, née Stephen (1882–1941), writer and essayist, co-founder of the Hogarth Press in 1917.

Virginia Woolf, originally named Adeline Virginia Stephen, is best known for her novels but also for her pioneering essays on literary history, art theory, women's writing and politics. She adopted the theory of stream of consciousness as a narrative device (first used by American philosopher and psychologist, William

James in 1890), describing the thoughts and feelings that go through the mind. Woolf is regarded as one of the most important modernist twentieth-century authors.

Virginia Woolf – A Brief Biography

Virginia Woolf, 1927

Virginia's father, the respected writer and critic, Sir Leslie Stephen died in 1904. Upon his death Virginia and her sister Vanessa moved from their childhood home at 22 Hyde Park Gate in Kensington to 46 Gordon Square in Bloomsbury, occupying the house from 1904 until 1907 along with their brothers Adrian and Thoby. This is where the Thursday evening meetings and the Bloomsbury Group began. These meetings were attended by Thoby Stephen's Cambridge friends that included: Leonard Woolf, Clive Bell, David Garnett, Duncan Grant, Lytton Strachey, John Maynard Keynes, Saxon Sidney-Turner and Roger Fry. Thursday evening discussion included taboo and controversial topics of the day such as sexual equality, politics and art. These meetings or parties were attended mainly by privileged upper- and middle-class intellectuals. Rejecting the traditional Victorian values that had been instilled in them as children, the group discussed and supported gay rights, uninhibited sexuality, open marriages, pacifism and women in the arts. Thoby contracted typhoid fever while on holiday in Greece and upon his return died at the age of 26 in 1906.

Clive Bell married Vanessa in 1907 and they continued to live at number 46 during their adulterous and open marriage. Eventually, after the Bells left, the economist John Maynard Keynes took over the house from 1916 until 1946.

In 1907, Adrian and Virginia moved to 29 Fitzroy Square in Fitzrovia. They continued to hold their ever increasingly popular evening parties until 1911. In 1910, Horace de Vere Cole, an Irish poet and prankster, instigated the famous Dreadnought Hoax, a prank in which Virginia and other members of the group dressed as a delegation of Ethiopian royals. They persuaded the English Royal Navy to show them around the warship HMS *Dreadnought*. Virginia spent a short period living at 38 Brunswick Square until 1912 and at 13 Clifford's Inn, near Chancery Lane in 1913.

In about 1900, Virginia was visiting her brother Thoby at Trinity College. Leonard Woolf was amongst the attendees and was attracted to Virginia instantly, however, nothing came of this. In 1909, Lytton Strachey proposed to Virginia, but the following day he withdrew his offer. Leonard Woolf was in Ceylon working as a civil servant. Strachey wrote to Leonard straightaway urging Leonard to propose to Virginia pointing out how compatible they would be together. 'Do you think Virginia would have me? Wire to me if she accepts. I'll take the next boat home,' replied Leonard. Virginia did not really know Leonard too well and found the idea quite amusing and did not even reply. Leonard returned to England two years later and rented rooms from Virginia and her brother Adrian in Brunswick Square. Shortly afterwards Leonard and Virginia were dating. Many proposals later Virginia agreed to marry Leonard.

In 1912, Virginia married Leonard Woolf in a civil ceremony held at St Pancras Central Register Office (Judd Street – now Camden Town Hall). By this time, Virginia was suffering from long periods of depression. Despite her illness she had started her first novel *The Voyage Out* in 1914 and, seeking a quieter life, they moved to Richmond upon Thames, in the same year.

Engagement photograph of Virginia and Leonard Woolf, 1912

The Hogarth Press

In 1915, the Woolf's purchased one half of Hogarth House on Paradise Road, Richmond upon Thames and by 1919 they owned the entire house. It was there that her depression lifted and they founded the Hogarth Press in 1917. The press was initially set up as a hobby, a means of relaxation from the mental stresses of writing. Virginia was very sensitive to criticism and disliked the stressful experience of submitting work to publishers. The Hogarth Press was an ideal solution.

The press was intended to free up censorship and avoid dealing with the frustrating editors of the time. Unsurprisingly, they published the works of members of the Bloomsbury Group and small experimental works that would have no commercial interest with larger publishers. The first publication from the press in 1917 was a pamphlet entitled *Two Stories* containing Virginia's story *The Mark on the Wall* and one by her husband called *Three Jews*. Other works by Virginia first published at Hogarth Press included: *Kew Gardens* (1919), *Monday or Tuesday* (1921) and the novel *Jacob's Room* (1922). It is believed that *Jacob's Room* was written partly as an elegy for her brother Thoby's death. The press encouraged new and interesting authors. This hobby eventually went on to publish works by E. M. Forster, Katherine Mansfield, Clive Bell, T. S. Eliot, Roger Fry and Sigmund Freud. Needless to say, it soon became a viable business.

In 1922, Virginia fell in love with a married woman, Vita Sackville-West, a writer, acclaimed poet and garden designer. Vita shared an open marriage, and Leonard also accepted this arrangement. The relationship ended around 1928 but they remained friends for life.

In 1924, the Woolfs took their press to Bloomsbury at 52 Tavistock Square, near to where Charles Dickens lived from 1851 to 1860. They lived on the top two floors with the Hogarth Press in the basement until 1939. Virginia continued to publish many of her novels at Tavistock Square including *To the Lighthouse* (1927), *A Room of One's Own* (1929), and *Mrs Dalloway* (1925). The press published a large amount of books from various notable authors ranging from Sigmund Freud's *The Future of an Illusion* (1928) to H. G. Wells' *Democracy Under Revision* (1927).

The couple briefly moved to the quieter Mecklenburgh Square in the east of Bloomsbury, but the house received bomb damage during the early London Blitz. The couple were afraid that if Germany invaded England Leonard, who was Jewish, would be in great danger. They agreed that if an invasion actually happened, they would commit suicide together.

In 1940, the couple decided that Monk's House, their retreat in the Sussex countryside (purchased in 1919), would offer a safer and more peaceful solution – Virginia never returned to London. In 1940, shortly after the Woolfs had moved out of London, No. 52, along with Tavistock Square, was virtually destroyed by a bomb. Fortunately, the printing press and some papers were salvaged and taken to Monk's House. The Tavistock Hotel now stands where this historic address once stood. However, by this time Virginia's mental health problems had become worse. Virginia wrote a suicide note to her husband explaining, 'I feel certain I am going mad again… I begin to hear voices, and I can't concentrate', and ending with 'I don't think two people could have been happier than we have been. V.' Virginia committed suicide by drowning herself in the River Ouse in March 1941 aged 59 years old. Her body was not found until three weeks later.

Virginia Woolf's modernist works such as *Mrs Dalloway* (1925), *Orlando* (1928), *To the Lighthouse* (1927), *A Room of One's Own* (1929), *The Waves* (1931) and *Between the Acts* (published posthumously in 1941) are examples of her stream of consciousness narrative technique of writing. Her peers and readers admired Virginia's surreal scenes mixed with intense storylines. Her essays reflected the Bloomsbury Group's way of thinking. There are many examples of Woolf's pioneering writing style. Virginia's essay *Modern Fiction* was originally published under the title *Modern Novels* in 1919. *Modern Fiction* criticises the previous generation of writers, guiding contemporary writers of fiction to write what they feel. The essay asks the writer to consider what is going on in the heads of their characters, not what editors, publishers and society expect from them.

Virginia Woolf's feminist texts, *A Room of One's Own* and *Three Guineas* (1938) led political and social outspokenness along with the rest of the Bloomsbury Group. Woolf and the group helped lead the way to modern thinking. Woolf admired and praised American writers who she felt were experimental and inventive unlike the tired and worn-out British literature of the day. She was influenced by writers such as poet, journalist, essayist and humanist Walter 'Walt' Whitman (1819–92) and practical philosopher, essayist and poet, Henry David Thoreau (1817–62). These and a few other American writers were popular with Virginia and her friends.

Shortly after Virginia's death, Leonard moved back to London. He had a brief stay in his old bomb-damaged home in Mecklenburgh Square, 'patching it up' as he put it. By October 1943, the poor conditions became unbearable and he took a lease at 24 Victoria Square in Westminster. During this time Leonard fell in love with Trekkie Parsons, the sister of one of Leonard's close friends, an affair that lasted for the rest of his life. Although married, Trekkie shared her time with Leonard and her husband who accepted this arrangement.

Leonard continued writing and published *After the Deluge* in 1953, his autobiography and *A Calendar of Consolation* in 1967. He also served on the Board of Directors for the *New Statesman* and continued to run his Hogarth Press and work in politics for the Labour Party. In 1964, Leonard was awarded an honorary doctorate from the University of Sussex and elected a fellow of the Royal Society of Literature in 1965. Leonard died in 1969, leaving Trekkie his entire estate and his manuscripts and publishing rights which she eventually donated to the University of Sussex. Leonard and Virginia's ashes were buried in the garden of Monk's House.

'Lock up your libraries if you like; but there is no gate, no lock, no bolt that you can set upon the freedom of my mind.'

Virginia Woolf: *A Room of One's Own* (1929)

EAST

Doughty Mews

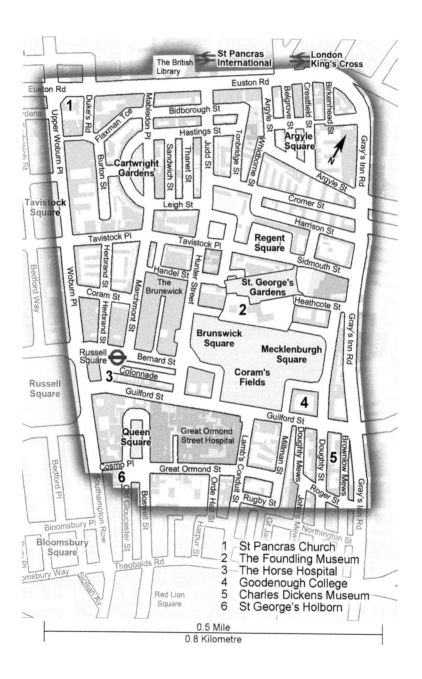

St Pancras International

London King's Cross

The British Library

Euston Rd

1 St Pancras Church
2 The Foundling Museum
3 The Horse Hospital
4 Goodenough College
5 Charles Dickens Museum
6 St George's Holborn

0.5 Mile
0.8 Kilometre

The northern part mainly comes under the ward of King's Cross with the exception of Marchmont Street and The Brunswick that sit in the Bloomsbury ward. The northernmost area around Argyle Square is a mix of nineteenth- and twentieth-century buildings and is predominantly working class and residential. However, there are many small, affordable hotels, and bed and breakfasts to be found here. Further south one comes across Regent Square Gardens before entering the more commercial and, in parts, affluent southern side. Continuing south, once one has crossed Guilford Street is the ward of Holborn and Covent Garden that contains the world famous Great Ormond Street Hospital and an abundance of medical institutions as well as unspoilt historic streets to explore.

The British Library – Euston Road

The British Library

Situated next door to St Pancras Station on Euston Road is a huge red or terracotta (depending on the light) complex. The British Library has been a Grade I listed building since 2015. The building is of brutalist architecture and is the largest twentieth-century public building constructed in the UK.

The British Library Act (the Act) of 1972 combined the nation's library institutions under one administrative umbrella, and in 1973, The British Library was born. This newly formed organisation needed a central, purpose-built building to manage and hold a comprehensive collection of books and other media. The Act gave The British Library Board the responsibility of ensuring that The British Library would serve as a national centre for reference and be available to the public and industry, educational institutions and libraries.

Many proposals for the new site were put forward, including one plan that would have meant demolishing a large area next to The British Museum. Eventually a site was agreed – a derelict goods yard next to St Pancras railway station and the Renaissance Hotel. A long planning process began and plans for the massive complex were drawn up by architect Sir Colin St John Wilson. The construction took two decades and was blighted by delays brought about by rising costs and political changes of the time. The library was officially opened by HM The Queen in 1998.

The building has a total floor area of over 112,000 square metres with fourteen floors: nine above ground and five floors below; there are eleven reading rooms and it holds over 150 million items to date (2018) with three million new items added yearly. The library receives a copy of every publication produced in the UK and Ireland. Its most treasured items include: the *Magna Carta*, *Lindisfarne Gospels*, Leonardo da Vinci's notebook, *The Times* first edition from 1788, the Beatles' manuscripts and a recording of Nelson Mandela's Rivonia trial speech. The King's Library tower holds books acquired by King George III which includes approximately 65,000 volumes of printed books and over 19,000 pamphlets. The *Gutenberg Bible* and other priceless collections are kept safely in the tower and are not accessible without special permission.

Holdings also range from: 3000-year-old Chinese oracle bones (the oldest items at The British Library) to an ongoing collection of almost every British and Irish newspaper since 1840. One will find 310,000 manuscripts ranging from Mary Shelley's *Frankenstein* to the Beatles' collection of work (lyrics, manuscripts and letters) and over 260,000 journals, 60 million patents and 4.5 million maps. The library has a northern site at Boston Spa, near Wetherby in Yorkshire that offers vast collections and research facilities.

The British Library constantly holds a wide variety of exhibitions and learning events throughout the year. During 2017 and 2018 The British Library held the highly successful *Harry Potter: A History of Magic* exhibition that moved on to New York in the latter part of 2018. Unlike the original Reading Room that existed in The British Museum, anyone who has a need to see specific items held at the library's collections may apply for a free reader pass. The public can pre-order items to read once registration has been accepted.

St Pancras Church – Euston Road

St Pancras Church and sculpture 'Alien'
by artist David Breuer-Weil

This hidden gem can often be overlooked as one makes a hasty retreat from the cascade of traffic on Euston Road to gain sanctuary in Tavistock Square Gardens, sit down and get one's bearings. The church is opposite Euston Station and reveals its columned entrance in Upper Woburn Place: St Pancras Church is a liberal Anglican place of worship and study. Often referred to as the 'new' St Pancras Church to distinguish it from the old St Pancras Church which is located on Pancras Road, a short walk north from St Pancras Station.

This humble and yet majestic Historic England Grade I church is of Greek revival architecture. Construction started in 1819 with the first stone laid by The Duke of York and was consecrated by the Bishop of London in 1822. The church was designed by local architect William Inwood and his son Henry William Inwood. During the time the building application for the church was accepted, Henry was in Athens where he brought back plaster casts and fragments to help enhance the architectural detail of the building. Inspiration was taken from the Acropolis in Athens focusing on two ancient Greek monuments – the Erechtheum and the Tower of the Winds. The Upper Woburn Place portico entrance has six Greek pillars and an octagonal tower above. The portico is similar to the Tower of the Winds and entices one to go in and look around. Stone female figures 'guarding the dead' stand above the north and south entrances to the Crypt. The Crypt houses a gallery that hosts a range of exhibitions and events throughout the year. Outside one will find some intriguing modern sculptures.

Cartwright Gardens

Cartwright Gardens

From Upper Woburn Place, Cartwright Gardens can be reached via Woburn Walk, a lane next to the Ambassadors Bloomsbury Hotel. Dominated by its tennis courts, this crescent garden is surrounded by Georgian hotels and guest houses. In spring the crescent awakens as residents and students from the University of London's Garden Halls of residence opposite come to enjoy the lively atmosphere the gardens have to offer.

Cartwright Gardens was originally known as Burton Crescent when it was constructed between 1809 and 1811. Burton Crescent was named after the architect James Burton (1761–1837) who was largely responsible for the development of the Bloomsbury district. The gardens were renamed Cartwright Gardens after political reformer and local resident John Cartwright (1740–1824). A bronze statue by George Clarke was erected in 1831 celebrating Cartwright's work as a reformer. Part of the inscription on the statue's plinth describes Cartwright as, 'The firm, consistent and persevering advocate of universal suffrage, equal representation, vote by ballot and annual parliaments.'

Cartwright Gardens is Bloomsbury's newest public space which opened to the public in 2016. The gardens contain some splendid specimens of the London plane tree which are famous for their khaki camouflage-patterned bark; half of London's trees are London planes.

Argyle Square and Garden

Argyle Square

This is a small neighbourhood garden just minutes walking distance from King's Cross Station and is a popular meeting place for young people. It has a full-size public basketball court and a playground. The diverse community, young and old, enjoy the park's lively, social and relaxing surroundings. The area has an abundance of small hotels serving the railway stations of King's Cross, St Pancras and Euston.

In the late 1800s the area around Argyle Square was depicted as 'semi-criminal to working class comfort' in Charles Booth's

London Poverty Map of 1889. Since the 1820s the area had not been very salubrious and was known for its prostitution until a major clean-up in the 1990s.

Regent Square Gardens

Regent Square Gardens

Surrounded by late twentieth-century blocks of flats on three sides, this garden is a community green space where residents walk their dogs or simply relax and chatter.

Regent Square Gardens was built around the 1820s and was originally intended for the private use of residents in the surrounding homes built in 1829. During the Second World War, a German V-1 flying bomb devastated a large part of the square. Today only the terraces on the south side remain. In 1995, the garden was sympathetically restored back, closely resembling the original design. A few of the original London plane trees remain in the garden today.

St George's Gardens

St George's Gardens, statue of Euterpe

Situated between Regent Square and Coram's Fields, the main entrance to this tranquil garden is from Handel Street. Other entrances link the garden to Sidmouth Street to the north-east and Heathcote Street to the south-east. The meandering pathways take one on a tour past flowerbeds, young couples meeting up for lunch, older residents chatting and putting the world to rights and dogs taking their owners for walks. A beautiful terracotta statue of Euterpe, the Muse of Instrumental Music, stands gracefully within the gardens.

St George's Gardens was purchased in 1713 and by 1714 was opened as a burial ground for St George's Bloomsbury and St George the Martyr Holborn (now simply called St George's Holborn). The gardens remain consecrated today. Burial grounds away from churches were almost unheard of in the early eighteenth century and this was one of the first. As the London population grew church burial grounds and yards began to overflow and the churches started to use what was then open country as burial grounds. The idea of being buried outside of a churchyard was not popular but in 1715, philanthropist and influential churchman Robert Nelson was laid to rest at St George's Gardens. This started a trend and ten years later there were an average of twenty burials a month. The granddaughter of Oliver Cromwell, Anna Gibson, was buried here in 1727. At this ground, they built a high wall to keep out body-snatchers who were supplying the nearby anatomy school. During the early 1800s the burial ground became overcrowded, and was eventually closed in 1855.

This part of Bloomsbury was poor and parks in the area were locked up to keep the poor lower-class people out, giving exclusive access to wealthy middle-class residents. The only outside spaces available to the poor were the old burial grounds. Miranda Hill, founder of the Kyrle Society and Octavia Hill, founder of the National Trust campaigned for 'outdoor sitting rooms' for the people. After a tough battle with the authorities the campaigns proved successful and in 1890 this disused burial ground was landscaped as a park and reopened to the public.

As time went by the gardens started to deteriorate. In 1997, the gardens received lottery funding allowing their restoration in 2001. The original wall with its grave stones are a reminder of its past. St George's Gardens is now a peaceful and relaxing place. The gardens are a well-kept community green space thanks to the relentless efforts of The Friends of St George's Gardens who proudly promote the gardens and work with Camden Council.

Mecklenburgh Square and Garden

Mecklenburgh Square

Formerly part of the Foundling Estate (explained later), Mecklenburgh Square and Garden lies to the east of Coram's Fields and consists of Goodenough College, a postgraduate residence and tall, formal Georgian houses. The smart houses in this quiet, mainly residential square look onto a tall well-trimmed hedge that surrounds the private garden. In spring the garden comes alive with crocuses and daffodils with several cherry trees providing bursts of pink blossom above. The London plane trees with their patchy brown and creamy white bark add depth, shade and character to the garden. Key holders, who include members of Goodenough College, can enjoy the garden and a game of tennis in the garden's court. Non-key holders have the opportunity to visit the garden on Open Garden Squares Weekend, every June.

Mecklenburgh Square and Garden were named after King George III's Queen, Charlotte of Mecklenburg-Strelitz (1744–1818). Construction started in 1804 and was not completed until around 1825. Architect Joseph Kay (1775–1847) designed the buildings around the eastern side of the square with the gardens completed around 1810 serving as a private centrepiece.

***

Amongst the many notable residents who lived around the square were: chemist Samuel Parkes (1761–1825) who died at No. 30 and mathematician Karl Pearson (1857–1936) who lived at No. 40 during his younger days from 1866 to 1875. Virginia Woolf lived at No. 37 from 1939 to 1940. The house was bombed in 1940 in a German air raid. This was Virginia's last London address before she opted for a quieter life at Monk's House in Sussex.

Goodenough College

Goodenough College

The William Goodenough House on the northern side of Mecklenburgh Square, and Goodenough College to the south, is an establishment which is a vibrant and pleasant residential accommodation building for postgraduates.

In 1930, Frederick Goodenough, Chairman of Barclays Bank wanted to create a halls of residence that would bring male students from parts of the British Empire together and promote international respect and understanding. Goodenough started a trust and opened London House that consisted of a few large houses in Mecklenburgh Place. The accommodation soon became full to the brim. From 1935, building commenced with the first of many phases at London House (between Guilford Street and Mecklenburgh Square). By 1957, the William Goodenough House for women and married students was completed and by 1991 both houses became mixed. Today, Goodenough College offers their residents who study at many of London's universities extra-curricular activities, events and a good social life that many refer to as a lifestyle.

Coram's Fields – The Foundling Hospital and Museum

This green parcel of land lying between The Brunswick and Mecklenburgh Square was once part of the Foundling Hospital Estate. From Guilford Street the area extends northwards to St George's Gardens. Just minutes from Great Ormond Street Hospital, this busy part of east Bloomsbury (especially at the Guilford Street side) tells a story of compassion and child welfare.

The Foundling Hospital

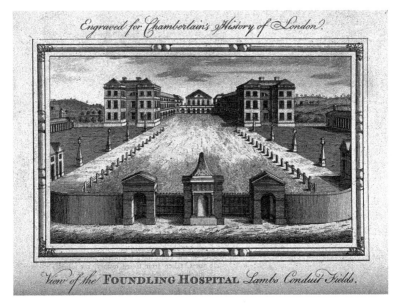

Foundling Hospital, 1770

The hospital was established in 1739 by sea captain and philanthropist Captain Thomas Coram (1668–1751) under Royal Charter granted by George II. Coram, who was born in Dorset, England, was sent to sea at only 11 years old. Coram as an adult lived in Taunton, Massachusetts where he started a successful shipbuilding business. He eventually gave land from a court settlement to build a schoolhouse on and helped found a Church of England in Taunton.

Coram returned to London in 1704 where he became involved in politics and spent many seafaring years earning the epithet of captain. At this time London, although a lively trading capital, was also very poor and disease ridden. Coram witnessed many children abandoned in the streets and started a seventeen-year campaign to set up a hospital that would care for and educate these unfortunate souls. His efforts were rewarded when, in 1739, he received a Royal Charter from King George II to establish his Foundling Hospital.

The governors of the hospital purchased fifty-six acres of land known then as Bloomsbury Fields from the Earl of Salisbury's Estate. The Foundling Hospital Estate was born and the hospital was built over five years, beginning in 1742. As intended the charity hospital cared for and educated unwanted children within the area. The estate consisted of far more land than was actually needed for the hospital and by the late eighteenth century, parts of the estate were developed into housing to raise much needed funds for the cash-strapped hospital. Helping the hospital to get established were the artist William Hogarth (1697–1764) and the composer George Frederic Handel (1685–1759). Hogarth donated some of his own work and encouraged other artists to do likewise. Handel donated an organ and conducted annual fundraising concerts in the hospital's chapel. This innovative charitable strategy made the hospital a desirable and fashionable venue that became the country's first public art gallery. By 1926, the hospital had to move due to changing social conditions, and to a certain extent pollution caused by the increase in population in the area. Children were moved to Redhill, Surrey; and later in 1935 were transferred to a new school in Berkhamsted, Hertfordshire. A statue of Thomas Coram stands outside The Foundling Museum in Brunswick Square.

The Sad Tale of the Marchmont Street Tokens

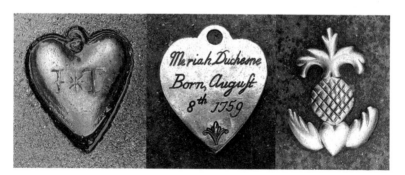

Marchmont Street, Foundling Tokens

Outside The Brunswick shopping centre, one may notice something quite baffling embedded into the pavements. Marchmont Street has an often missed art installation created by artist John Aldus. Installed in 2010, metal objects known as tokens draw one towards the entrance of The Foundling Hospital Museum.

This sad trail represents objects that were left by mothers when leaving their child in the care of The Foundling Hospital. Mothers were asked to label their children by written form or any other method to distinguish them as their own. This identification system ensured that the child was reunited to the rightful mother once care was no longer deemed necessary.

Between the 1740s and 1760s the identity system involved cutting a piece of fabric from the child's clothes and then cutting it in half. One half was attached to the child's admission record that held a unique admission number and the other piece of fabric given to the mother as a form of receipt. In order to return the child to the mother once care had ended, the mother was expected to recite the date her child was admitted and hand over the piece of matching fabric. To allow for the mother losing the fabric receipt or forgetting their child's admission date, mothers would leave a unique item with the child, such as a token as additional identification. These tokens were placed and sealed inside the admission billet and were never opened unless the child was claimed. The tokens were made from items ranging from jewellery to coins and often contained personalised poems. Mothers often incorporated needlework and inscribed medallions. A popular form of identification were pennies with personalised engravings on them. It is sad to think that an unclaimed child would never see this token of hope from their mother. During the mid-nineteenth century, the unclaimed billets were opened and a selection put on display in the hospital. The original tokens are now on display at The Foundling Hospital Museum. Evenly and neatly isolated behind glass, these tiny unclaimed tokens, many marked with loving messages, are indeed orphans themselves.

How long the pavement art installation will exist I do not know, probably for as long as the artist and sponsors can keep replacing the replicas. Look down, tread carefully, and spare a thought for those unfortunate little souls.

Coram's Fields

Coram's Fields

Shielded from the busy Guilford Street by the remaining remnants of the original Foundling Hospital that once stood here lies a seven-acre playground that is free to enter. This kid's kingdom has a simple rule – no adult can enter without a child – and offers sand pits and a duck pond, while goats, rabbits and other adorable animals inhabit pet's corner. A café and nursery also lie within this wonderland.

A plaque at the entrance reads: 'The site of The Foundling Hospital established in 1739 by Captain Thomas Coram were offered for sale as building land in 1926 when owing to changing social conditions the old hospital was sold and demolished.'

Once the land had been purchased by developer James White, the hospital was demolished and only the single storey Georgian buildings remain today. White had plans to transfer Covent Garden Market to the site but, fiercely opposed by local residents, the plan never materialised.

The governors of The Foundling Hospital and the Education Committee of the London County Council together with donations from many supporters realised the opening of Coram's Fields in 1936. Pioneer of popular journalism, owner of Associated Newspapers Ltd and a supporter of Nazi Germany, Harold Harmsworth, First Viscount Rothermere (1868–1940) made a large donation towards the playground's future.

Today, Coram's Fields are run by an independent charitable trust called Coram's Fields and the Harmsworth Memorial Playground, which keeps this unique playground alive and kicking.

The Foundling Museum

Opened to the public in 2004, The Foundling Museum is situated in a cul-de-sac at the north end of Brunswick Square, on part of the site of the former Foundling Hospital. The building was constructed in the 1930s, and has architectural features from the original eighteenth-century hospital and a statue of Thomas Coram outside, seated looking towards The Brunswick. The thought-provoking Foundling Museum is dedicated to the former hospital. Here one will discover the nationally important Foundling Hospital Art Collection as well as the Gerald Coke Handel Collection (the world's greatest private collection relating to Handel and his musical contemporaries). The museum highlights The Foundling Hospital's charity work for children and exhibits objects and archive documents that tell the story of the hospital. This charity work continues today through the childcare organisation Coram based in Brunswick Square.

Brunswick Square and Gardens

Brunswick Square Gardens and the Brunswick plane tree

With The Brunswick residential and shopping centre peering through the foliage this spacious, well-maintained garden has a variety of trees and shrubs that contrast with each other. The gardens have plenty of open space and ample seating to take a respite between visiting The Brunswick and The Foundling Museum, Coram's Fields or Marchmont Street.

Brunswick Square and Gardens was named in honour of Caroline of Brunswick (1768–1821) who was born in Braunschweig (Brunswick) Germany. Caroline was married to King George III's eldest son, George and was Princess of Wales from 1795 to 1820. Upon King George III's death Caroline became Queen consort to King George IV from 1820 until her death in 1821. George who was heavily in debt only agreed to marry Caroline Princess of Brunswick in order to gain a parliamentary increase in his allowance (they separated shortly after they married but never divorced).

Caroline was very unpopular with the royal family due to her poor behaviour that often embarrassed the king and royal family, however, she was very popular with the general public. In a bid to divorce his estranged wife the king accused her of adultery. Caroline was the only British Queen to be tried for adultery in 1820 but, to add insult to injury to the king, she won the case. Queen Caroline died the following year and was laid to rest back in Braunschweig with the words 'the Injured Queen of England' inscribed on her coffin.

The gardens were built as recreation grounds along with Coram's Fields for The Foundling Hospital. James Burton was commissioned by The Foundling Hospital governors to develop the square and gardens. In 1790, the Foundling Estate leased part of its land for housebuilding to raise funds for the hospital, the area included Brunswick and Mecklenburgh Squares. Houses were constructed around Brunswick Square between 1795 and 1802. The square and gardens were not considered highly fashionable, but respectable in the 1800s.

As time went by sadly all the original Georgian houses were replaced by modern buildings, though the garden was refurbished by Camden Council between 2002 and 2003. A London plane tree which was planted in 1796, thought to be the second oldest in London, stands in the grounds.

***

J. M. Barrie, author and playwright (1860–1937), lived at 8 Grenville Street (demolished in 1938) on the south-west corner of the square from 1885 to 1888. He did not write Peter Pan while lodging here, but was most certainly influenced by Bloomsbury and Brunswick Squares in his novel and play.

For a very short time around the first decade of the 1900s, the square became popular with the Bloomsbury Group. Former residents of the vicinity included: John Ruskin, E. M. Forster,

John Leech and Michael Wishart. No. 38 was the house that Virginia and Leonard Woolf, and Adrian Stephen shared with Maynard Keynes and Duncan Grant from 1911 to 1912. The writer, art critic and philanthropist, John Ruskin (1819–1900) was born at 54 Hunter Street, Brunswick Square.

Marchmont Street

Marchmont Street

At first sight this popular and slightly worn street seems reminiscent of any British shopping street. This is where the locals do their day-to-day shopping, but it is not as simple as that, because this is Marchmont Street. The street runs from Cartwright Gardens to Bernard Street where Russell Square tube station lies. The street is known as a bookworm's paradise and for its ground-breaking mixed-used development, The Brunswick. This relatively calm street has a lot to boast about and starts with a compelling history.

By the mid-1700s, Thomas Coram's Foundling Hospital was established and surrounded by fields. In 1790, the Foundling Estate made the decision to build houses on its land. The wealthy residents of Great Ormond Street were opposed to the plans, claiming that it would spoil their view of Hampstead and Highgate. By the early 1800s, houses had been built on the Foundling Estate of which James Burton played a major role, including Everett Street (now the south part of Marchmont Street). By 1813, the Skinners' Estate to the north and the Foundling Estate had been developed with Marchmont Street extended to Bernard Street by 1878. Marchmont Street was named after one of the governors of The Foundling Hospital, Alexander Hume Campbell (1675–1740), 2nd Earl of Marchmont.

The Foundling Estate who owned the land had banned any non-residential use of property on their estate until, due to public demand, they permitted a flexible zoning policy. By 1811, Marchmont Street and Kenton Street became commercial and Marchmont Street became Bloomsbury's high street. From the early 1900s onwards, redevelopment started to take place that included purpose-built retail units, offices and accommodation. Many of the shops in Marchmont Street were often visited by members of the Bloomsbury Group, including Virginia Woolf (who did her shopping here). In 1958, the Foundling Estate sold eleven acres of land to developers who, after demolishing many Georgian terraced houses, completed The Brunswick in 1972.

The Brunswick

The Brunswick

As one walks southwards down Marchmont Street a huge low-rise structure reveals itself, like a large, white cruise liner moored in its port, with the shopping precinct on its deck. Taking up half of Marchmont Street in length and reaching Brunswick Square in width, this is indeed a very big structure. On a sunny day the building takes on a bright and airy, almost Mediterranean character. This magnificent piece of late 1960s brutalist architecture is known today as The Brunswick.

Built by McAlpine and Sons on the site of demolished Georgian and Victorian terraces, The Brunswick (known previously as Brunswick Centre) was named after Brunswick Square opposite. The Brunswick is a residential and shopping centre designed by the architect Patrick Hodgkinson (1930–2016).

The story began when investor and developer Alec Coleman purchased land from the Foundling Estate in 1958 and set up

Marchmont Properties to manage the proposed development. Marchmont Properties were partly financed by building contractors Robert McAlpine and Sons who eventually took over the project from Coleman. The first sketches for The Brunswick were conceived in 1959 and by 1968 the final working drawings were ready. The architect's intention was to create a 'low-rise modern city village' consisting of two parallel blocks of stepped design that would welcome light into the flats and shopping street in-between.

The development was planned for private mixed use and was a fairly new concept in the 1960s. However, in 1964 the newly elected Labour Party lead by Harold Wilson passed new laws to rehouse evicted tenants. In 1966, Camden Council signed a ninety-nine-year lease on the residential part of the building while ownership of the structure and shopping areas remained with the developer. This new law forced a radical rethink as buyers for the planned upmarket penthouses pulled out not wanting to share the building with council tenants. The original 'private mixed' plans were immediately scrapped at the insistence of the council's wishes to provide one- and two-bedroom apartments and bedsits.

Construction took five years and was completed in 1972. During this time the design process went through many changes between local authorities and the client. The cheaper and compromised building was handed over to Camden Council and the developer but had difficulties attracting retailers. The intended finishing touches had been omitted in a bid to save money and the grey concrete structure was unpainted. The council could not afford to paint the exterior that Hodgkinson would have painted cream, as homage to the Georgian terraced homes that once stood on the site.

For a long time quite a few retail premises were unoccupied and the centre looked tired and run down and needed a face-lift. During this period the freehold ownership changed hands a few times, but was eventually purchased by Allied London Properties in 1998 who saw potential in Hodgkinson's masterpiece. In 2000, the grey, unpainted and often disliked piece of modernist architecture achieved Grade II listed status.

Allied London Properties hired Patrick Hodgkinson to revise his original plans and in turn architects Levitt Bernstein were commissioned and a £22 million renovation project started in 2002. The blocks were finally painted cream and artist Susanna Heron designed water features for the central space. The renovation was completed in 2006. Retailers were queuing up to be a part of the bright and airy, newly-branded building called The Brunswick.

In 2014, Lazari Investments Limited purchased the freehold of the building, which includes all the 560 residential flats, and car parking below the shopping centre. The residential side is a mixture of social housing and flats; Camden Council has sold off a proportion of units to private owners on a long-term leasehold basis. The Brunswick has shops and a supermarket, cafés, restaurants and a Curzon cinema. It is a bright and cheerful mixed-use community that now lives up to its original intended purpose.

Bloomsbury Festival

Upon opening the newly renovated Brunswick in 2006, Allied London wanted to mark this special occasion in style. They commissioned Roma Backhouse, a local cultural organiser, to set up an event to celebrate the area and The Brunswick's new lease of life. The event was an instant success and the Bloomsbury Festival was born. When Allied London sold The Brunswick in 2008 the funding came to a halt. Backhouse and Festival Producer Maddy Jones, through their company Hidden Cities, found a new collection of funding partners from across the Bloomsbury area. They also received a large anonymous donation that ensured the festival's future. By 2010, the festival was back on its feet and from that year onwards it has proven to be a cultural asset of Bloomsbury. The festival is spread all over Bloomsbury, with academic and cultural institutions celebrating creativity and achievement. The many live performances and events around the squares highlight Bloomsbury's diversity and cultural impact that this small part of London has to offer. The festival runs for five days every October with a different theme each year: 2018 was, Activists and Architects of Change.

The Marquis Cornwallis – Public House

On the corner of Coram Street and Marchmont Street opposite The Brunswick one will find a friendly pub that is enjoyed by locals and tourists alike. The pub was named after the celebrated British General of the American Revolution Charles Cornwallis, 1st Marquess Cornwallis (1738–1805). The Marquis Cornwallis was opened in 1806, however, the current building dates from the early 1900s and is still going strong today. The public house was reported to have been visited by singer Sandi Shaw and American actor and musician Jack Lemmon. Rumour has it that the Kray brothers would pop in for a pint here in the 1970s.

Lord John Russell – Public House

At the north end of Marchmont Street near Cartwright Gardens stands a lively public house, painted deep blue, with pavement benches and a side entrance once used for horse-drawn deliveries. The public house that used to be a distillery was named after Lord John Russell who was twice Prime Minister from 1846 to 1852, and again from 1865 to 1866. He was also an advocate of the 1832 Reform Act. Charles Dickens dedicated *A Tale of Two Cities* to Russell who was a close friend. The first pint was served in the 1850s and the landlord was a Mr John Russell (no relation). A pub named after a politician, what next?!

***

Famous former residents of Marchmont Street include: artist and lithographer John Skinner Prout who lived at No. 43 between 1838 and 1840, and at No. 41 watercolour artist William Henry Hunt from 1825 to 1845. Vladimir Lenin briefly lived just around the corner in Tavistock Place in 1908 and American writer and researcher of anomalous phenomena Charles Fort stayed at No. 39A from 1921 to 1928. Comedian and Actor Kenneth

Williams lived at No. 57 above his father's hairdressing shop from 1935 to 1956. Saville Row originated from here when James Poole started a linen draper's business at 6 Everett Street in 1806, known now as 11 Marchmont Street. The Marchmont Association have proudly placed blue plaques, on the houses, celebrating the street's famous former residents. Marchmont Street remained a traditional high street into the 1960s.

Today, the street has a variety of shops: greengrocers, takeaways, cafés, hairdressers, dry cleaners and a DIY store. There are also various estate agents who are partly responsible for the attempt to re-brand Bloomsbury as 'Mid-Town'.

Bookshops of Marchmont Street

Skoob Books

I would like to focus on what Marchmont Street is mostly respected for: independent booksellers, and whom are amongst the finest in London. I will walk you from north to south to whet your appetite. One will find oneself spoilt for choice when it comes to variety, so allow plenty of time.

Collinge & Clark

At the north end of Marchmont Street by Cartwright Gardens in Leigh Street one will discover Collinge & Clark where the television series *Black Books* was filmed. This inviting old-fashioned looking shop was founded in 1989 and specialises in rare and second-hand books, as well as private presses, graphic design and typography. The shop also stocks a wide range of affordable titles in its dark interior and outside at the front of the shop.

Judd Books

In 1992, this was a small shop in Judd Street before moving to the north end of Marchmont Street at No. 82. The shop is packed with second-hand and discounted new books, and it is crammed ceiling high on both floors with the widest range of books one could wish to find. The considerate owner has supplied stepladders so that one can reach the upper shelves.

The School of Life

At No. 70 is a global learning centre that teaches pragmatic philosophy and lifestyle self-realisation. In 2008, Alain de Botton together with other like-minded individuals co-founded The School of Life. The range of books and products for sale in their smart shop relates to the courses they offer. They are glad to give advice to help you find books that suit your personal needs. The shop runs courses and events on all manner of lifestyle subjects from working life to love and family. This is a fun place to learn about life and its challenges from the books on offer.

Gay's The Word

This shop was established back in 1979 and is the UK's first LGBT bookstore and was featured in the 2014 film *Pride*, directed by Matthew Warchus. They are the only specifically lesbian and gay book specialists in the UK. This pioneering shop at No. 66 sells a large range of books that go beyond the mainstream. The shop is known for its friendly community approach to all and their regular events and discussion meetings.

Skoob Books

Skoob was founded in the 1970s and moved to its current premises in 2005. Skoob Books are an independent bookseller that specialise in affordable second-hand books (one of London's widest ranges). They are located in the north end of The Brunswick at 66 The Brunswick, off Marchmont St. This delightful shop with its helpful, friendly staff boasts 2000 square feet (186 metre^2) of space containing 55,000 different titles. They have a warehouse in Oxfordshire that has an ever-growing stock of over a million pre-owned books which are steadily being catalogued. The shop also stocks local interest books and posters of front covers. There is a piano in the music section, giving one the opportunity to play your music books before you buy!

***

The Horse Hospital – Arts Venue

The Horse Hospital

South of Marchmont Street and around the corner from Russell Street tube station in Colonnade (a street) one will come across an arts venue, The Horse Hospital. The Victorian exterior has hints of its original bronze London brick beneath the sooty grime that has built up over the years.

The Horse Hospital did not start its life as a modern arts venue. The original building was built in 1797 by James Burton and was possibly redeveloped after the 1860s. The name of the building is not without resonance: before it became an arts venue sick horses were cared for here, and inside there are little reminders such as iron pillars and tethering rings.

Founded in 1992 by fashion designer, collector and film art director Roger K. Burton, the Horse Hospital took its present-day form as an independent arts venue in 1993. In the same year, the Vive Le Punk! Exhibition took place, which showcased the original clothes and items designed by Vivienne Westwood and Malcolm McLaren for their rebellious Kings Road shops during the 1970s. Since then the venue has seen many independent and progressive exhibitions, ranging from art and film to fashion, literature and music.

The Horse Hospital is well known for its archive of rare films, performances and underground artists, alternative musicians and fashion designers. The venue has ties with the British Film Institute, the Victoria and Albert Museum, the Hayward Gallery and the Barbican Centre. The venue has international recognition from many organisations such as the Brooklyn Museum of Modern Art and the Shishedo Gallery in Tokyo. The organisers are constantly on the lookout for artists who practice outside the mainstream. The Grade II listed Horse Hospital building operates a not for profit policy and has space for hire.

Queen Square and Gardens

Queen Square Gardens

Surrounded by an assortment of medical establishments and buildings of contrasting architectural styles; this attractive square garden is an ideal place to take refuge. St George the Martyr Holborn church sits at the south-western side of the square looking out across a paved pedestrian seating area and onto Great Ormond Street. Professionals and people coming to or from their medical appointments use this leafy retreat to catch a moment's solitude. The well-maintained and relaxing square garden is located between Southampton Row (Russell Square) and Great Ormond Street Hospital.

Queen Square was originally named Devonshire Square and was set out around 1706; it was later renamed Queen Anne's Square. The square was previously named Queen Anne's Square because of a statue located within the gardens; however, the statue is now believed to be of Queen Charlotte the wife of King George III who was king from 1760 to 1820. It was built on land that was owned by the Curzon family of Kedleston.

During 1713 to 1725, houses were built around three sides of the square leaving the north side undeveloped, giving residents a good view of Hampstead and Highgate. By the end of the eighteenth century, The Foundling Hospital, in heavy debt yet owner of the land to the north of the square, decided to develop a small estate. The new houses facing Queen Square were given a grand façade as a concession to angry residents opposed to their view being blocked. In 1797, the Curzons also came into financial difficulties and started selling the freeholds of many of the square's houses allowing residents to, within reason, run their businesses from home. The square was becoming a less fashionable area and the upper classes moved further west and eventually French refugees moved in. By the nineteenth century, the area became more mixed-class and charitable institutions became established such as the Roman Catholic Aged Poor Society and the Italian Hospital that provided medical care for poor Italians.

Queen Square from Ackermann's Repository of Arts, 1812

Eventually hospitals and various medical institutions took over the large homes surrounding Queen Square Gardens and today the entire square is home to the likes of The National Hospital for

Neurology and Neurosurgery, and part of University College London, providing research and medical care.

In 1915, a Zeppelin bomb hit the square and exploded. It was believed that over a thousand people were sleeping in the surrounding buildings that night but, incredibly, no one was injured. A tiny plaque in the park marks the spot where the bomb fell.

Queen Square

***

Notable past residents of this square include: physician Sir William Browne between 1749 and 1774, and the inventor of electric telegraphy Francis Ronalds between 1820 and 1822. Many interesting people and institutions have occupied the square, from its upper class beginnings to middle-class professionals, and today's excellent medical institutions. The square offers a good central respite from visiting the museums or after a bit of retail therapy in The Brunswick.

The Queen's Larder – Public House

According to legend, The Queen's Larder was a cellar rented by Queen Charlotte to store food for the king who stayed at the square during treatment for mental illness. The actual Queen's Larder building dates from 1710, and is situated next to St George the Martyr Holborn church.

St George the Martyr Holborn (St George's Holborn)

St George's Holborn

This happy and welcoming church has a light, airy and relaxing café that serves excellent coffee, teas, fresh salads and gorgeous pastries. One can sit and drink coffee while reading a book within the nave! The church offers refuge from the hustle and bustle of Southampton Row and Great Ormond Street. Easily recognised by its zinc spire and gothic elements, St George's Holborn is an Anglican church located at the south end of Queen Square. In order to distinguish it from St George's Bloomsbury the church was named St George's Holborn. The two churches shared a burial ground now known as St George's Gardens (see St George's Gardens section).

The church was often nicknamed the chimney-sweeps' church, because they held charity dinners for chimney sweeps over the Christmas period. The church was built between 1703 and 1706 by Arthur Tooley, and later bought by the Commission for Building Fifty New Churches and in 1723 became a parish church. J. B. Papworth remodelled the church in the early nineteenth century adding a bell-tower and two frontages. Later, between 1867 and 1869, architect Samuel Sanders Teulon changed the exterior by adding the present-day columns and a unique roof. In 1951, the church was designated a Grade II* listed building. English poet and children's writer Ted Hughes and American poet Sylvia Plath married at this church in 1956.

Great Ormond Street

East side of Great Ormond Street

Known for the world famous hospital and its institutes, the western end of the street is a hive of activity as families, patients and ambulances go about their business. The eastern end of the street takes on a calmer atmosphere and character: Georgian terraces displaying flowers in window boxes and potted plants near the intersection of Lamb's Conduit Street welcome one to the peaceful side of Great Ormond Street.

Great Ormond Street Hospital – 'The Child First and Always'

Behind Queen Square along Great Ormond Street, one will find this large hospital as well as other medical institutions. The entire area has been built and added to for years so, as one can imagine, it is a mixture of traditional and contemporary buildings.

After a lengthy campaign by physician Dr Charles West (1816–98) The Hospital for Sick Children was founded in 1852 as the first hospital dedicated to children in England. The hospital opened with just ten beds, eventually becoming a world leader in children's hospitals with Queen Victoria's patronage. Charles Dickens was one of the hospital's first fundraisers, saving the hospital from its first major financial crisis. In 1858, Dickens spoke at a fundraiser and gave a public reading of *A Christmas Carol* at St. Martin-in-the-Field's church which helped raise enough money to purchase a neighbouring house on Great Ormond Street.

By the end of the century the hospital had grown and developed to include a nursing school, a private nursing service and a medical school. In 1929, J. M. Barrie donated the rights to *Peter Pan* to Great Ormond Street Hospital. Barrie claimed that Peter Pan had been a patient at the hospital, commenting, 'It was he who put me up to the little thing I did for the hospital.' In 1938, the modern and advanced Southwood Building opened and in 1946 the UCL Institute of Child Health was founded by Professor Alan Moncrieff.

By 1947, the first heart and lung unit was founded by Mr David Waterston and Dr Richard Bonham-Carter and by 1951 The Children's Hospital School opened, beginning with only one teacher.

In 1962, David Waterson and his team established the first children's heart and lung bypass machine. The 1970s and 1980s saw pioneering advances in children's medical treatment and care, from heart and lung transplants to cancer research and treatment (with the first bone marrow transplant by Professor Roland Levinsky in 1979).

Diana, Princess of Wales (1961–97), became President of the hospital in 1989 until her death. Her valued service to the hospital is commemorated by a bust in the lobby of the hospital's chapel and a plaque at the entrance of the hospital.

Rhys Evans in 2001 became the first child in the UK, and one of the first in the world, to receive gene therapy treatment at Great Ormond Street Hospital. From 2000 onwards, the hospital continued with medical firsts and outstanding treatments built upon its past practices. Great Ormond Street Hospital Charity helps to fund refurbishment, research, equipment, accommodation and other support services for children and their families.

Doughty Street

Doughty Street

Doughty Street has a calm residential ambience, with rows of tall Georgian houses that were built around 1790 to 1840 and is lined with trees. Today, barrister's chambers, accountants and business management companies occupy some of the houses. The Doughty Street Chambers at No. 54 is praised for their commitment to defending freedom and civil liberties. Since their foundation in 1990, they have become one of the largest sets in the UK with over 120 members.

The Charles Dickens Museum

This house gives one a fascinating insight into part of the life of the great author. Taking out a three-year lease, Charles Dickens (1812–70) and his wife Catherine lived at 48 Doughty Street from 1837 until 1839. Dickens spent some of his most productive years at Doughty Street where he wrote *Oliver Twist*, *The Pickwick Papers* and *Nicholas Nickleby*. The Victorian family home offers a window into his private life that contains his study, desk and handwritten drafts from the novels he wrote.

Charles Dickens circa 1860s

Dickens' wife's younger sister, Mary Hogarth, died in this house at the age of seventeen in Dickens' arms in 1837. The traumatic experience rendered Dickens unable to write for a month. Dickens and his wife had two daughters at No. 48: Mary (who was named after Mary Hogarth) and Kate. Despite the untimely death of Mary Hogarth, bringing up a family and being occupied with work, they regularly found time to entertain many leading figures of the day.

***

Between Guilford Street and Theobalds Road, one will discover many typical Georgian terraces. Great James Street and Rugby Street are good examples of a less busy London, with the traditional Rugby Tavern offering one the opportunity to take a rest before exploring central Bloomsbury.

The Rugby Tavern

NORTH CENTRAL
(THE UNIVERSITY DISTRICT)

Senate House Library, University of London

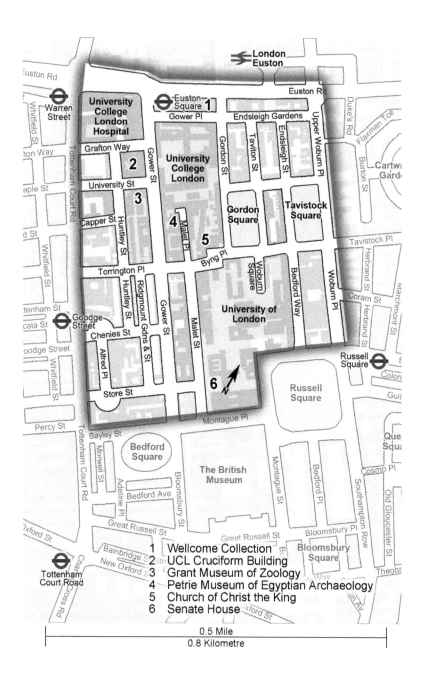

London Euston

Euston Rd

Euston Rd

Warren Street

University College London Hospital

Gower Pl

Euston Square 1

Endsleigh Gardens

Grafton Way

2

University St

University College London

Gordon St

Taviton St

Endsleigh St

Upper Woburn Pl

Duke's Rd

Flaxman Tce

Burton St

Cartw Gard

3

Capper St

Huntley St

Malet Pl

Gordon Square

Tavistock Square

Tavistock Pl

Herbrand St

Marchmont St

4

5

Byng Pl

Torrington Pl

Huntley St

Ridgmount Gdns & St

Gower St

Woburn Square

Bedford Way

Woburn Pl

Coram St

Herbrand St

Goodge Street

Chenies St

University of London

6

Russell Square

Russell Square

Colon

Alfred Pl

Store St

Montague Pl

Guil

Percy St

Bayley St

Bedford Square

Morwell St

Adeline Pl

Bedford Ave

Bloomsbury St

The British Museum

Montague St

Bedford Pl

Southampton Row

Old Gloucester St

Que Squa

Cosmo Pl

Great Russell St

Great Russell St

Bloomsbury Pl

Bloomsbury Square

Theoba

Oxford St

Bainbridge S

New Oxford S

1 Wellcome Collection
2 UCL Cruciform Building
3 Grant Museum of Zoology
4 Petrie Museum of Egyptian Archaeology
5 Church of Christ the King
6 Senate House

Tottenham Court Road

Charing Cross Rd

Oxford St

0.5 Mile
0.8 Kilometre

Welcome to the heart of London's most famous university district. The entire central part of Bloomsbury can only be described as one big open campus, shared mainly by the University of London with Senate House Library as its iconic beacon, and University College London (UCL).

UCL, Malet Place South Quad

Malet Street and Gower Street

Beginning at Montague Place, this is a good place to experience the energy that the district emits. Malet Street takes one past well-known establishments such as Senate House Library, Birkbeck (University of London), and the world famous Royal Academy of Dramatic Art (RADA). The street crosses over Torrington Place and becomes Malet Place, that leads one into the heart of UCL's campus. Within most of the campuses, visitors are free to wander and enter some of the buildings including the parts of Senate House Library where the general public may apply for library membership, ranging from one day up to a year. The UCL even promotes self-guided tours around their campus.

One will soon discover that both universities started life as one in Gower Street, and have a complex history that I will outline briefly. Both the University of London and UCL deserve further reading to appreciate their remarkable histories and contributions to the world. Both universities are responsible for the development of Bloomsbury's medical district (see The Hospital and Medical Quarter – Gower Street area).

London University – 1826–36

London University, coloured engraving

Nineteenth-century London, the capital of the first industrial nation and the British Empire, had everything except a university. For many years, people had voiced their opinion that London needed a university. It was traditionally accepted that Oxford and Cambridge educate with 'godliness and good learning' while London nurtures enterprise and careers.

Breaking away from tradition, the London University is where it all began for Bloomsbury and, indeed, London. From day one the university was leading the way in religious tolerance and equal opportunities. The University of London started life in Gower Street as London University, and then moved away, only to return almost next door to Malet Street many years later.

This table shows briefly how University of London evolved.		
Years	**London University**	**Status**
1826–1836	London University founded in 1826. First academic classes held in 1828. Changed its name in 1836 to University of London. Location: Gower Street.	Owned jointly by shareholders (unincorporated). Only permitted to award Certificates of Honours.
1836–1937	University of London Location: Various locations around London. Note: a newly formed UCL remained in the Gower Street building.	Royal Charters in 1836 and 1837 permitted them to award degrees to its affiliated colleges and schools including UCL. University of London Act 1898 made it responsible for their institutions in 1900 and became a federal university.
1937–present	Returns to Bloomsbury Senate House.	Became a global university.

The Foundations – 1826–28

There is a common misconception that the philosopher and founder of utilitarianism and social reformer Jeremy Bentham (1748–1832) founded the self-styled London University in Gower Street. By the time London University had opened to its students in 1828 Bentham was an 80-year-old man. What he did do was to give his unconditional and financial support towards the founding of London's first university making him the auto-icon of today's UCL.

Jeremy Bentham – Ahead of His Time

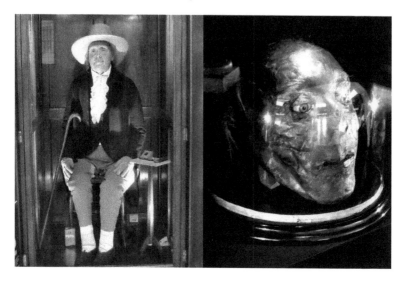

Jeremy Bentham's dressed skeleton and mummified head

Shortly before his death, Bentham requested that his skeleton should be preserved and dressed in his own clothes with a replacement wax head. He can usually be found in a glass-fronted cabinet in UCL's South Cloisters – yes, you read correctly! His mummified head is kept in the college safe.

'The said truth is that it is the greatest happiness of the greatest number that is the measure of right and wrong.'

Jeremy Bentham: *A Fragment on Government* (1776).

The Foundations – A Poet and a Lawyer

Thomas Campbell (left) and Henry Brougham (right)

During a visit to Bonn, Germany in 1820 Scottish poet Thomas Campbell (1777–1844), was highly impressed with their university's religious tolerance. On Campbell's return he formulated the idea of establishing a 'great' London university based around 'effective and multifarious' teaching, rewarding learners with Honours in the Arts and Sciences. In 1825, Campbell wrote an open letter in *The Times* newspaper to fellow Scot, Henry Brougham (1778–1868) a lawyer, British Whig Party politician, utilitarian and reformer who later became Lord Chancellor of England. Campbell's letter expressed his ideas of a great London university. Despite some fierce opposition Brougham, who was renowned as a doer, made it happen. With Brougham's guidance and the help of a few others, the poet and the lawyer laid the foundation of the London University.

At this time, England only had two universities, Oxford and Cambridge. Jeremy Bentham described them as 'the two great public nuisances' and as 'storehouses and nurseries of political corruption'. Both universities only accepted students who were members of the Church of England.

The idea for an 'all welcome' London university was embraced by many social groups, and soon attracted financiers prepared to support the idea. One financier was Jewish millionaire and political activist Isaac Lyon Goldsmid (1778–1859) who ensured the Jewish community's full support.

Land had been bought in Bloomsbury by the wealthiest supporters for the university and in 1825 the land was ready to hand over to the university to build on. In 1826, after a year of public and private meetings chaired by Brougham, a deed of settlement was signed and shares costing £100 each were issued to raise funds. The university would stay true to its principle that religion should not be an entry requirement or be a taught subject.

Construction started on the London University on Gower Street in 1826 under the architect William Wilkins (1778–1839), who is best known for designing the National Gallery in Trafalgar Square. His neo-Grecian design of the university is regarded as his finest work.

The London University took its first academic classes in 1828. It was now up and running; however, ever since 1826 the promoters wanted a Royal Charter that would allow the university to grant degrees instead of Certificates of Honours. After years of fierce parliamentary debate and the negative influences of both the Tories and Oxford and Cambridge universities, who labelled it as a 'godless cockney' university, Parliament finally approved Royal Charters in 1836 and 1837.

The Separation – 1836–37

The charters allowed the London University to award degrees to its students and affiliated colleges, and changed its name to University of London. In 1837, the University of London (UL) now a separate entity moved out of Gower Street leaving a newly formed UCL behind in the Gower Street building. The UL took up residence in apartments at Somerset House in Covent Garden until 1853 followed by three more temporary locations. Eventually the university moved into a purpose-built building in Burlington Gardens, Mayfair, from 1870 until 1900. Burlington Gardens were used mainly for administration and had examination halls that served the UL's colleges and institutions.

In 1878, the UL became the first university in the UK to admit women for degrees; however, during this period the university was being criticised as only really serving as an administration, exam and awarding body. There was a demand for a 'proper' teaching university in London.

Eventually, the University of London Act 1898 was passed, and by 1900 the UL had a federal structure, making it responsible for their institutions. The responsibilities included monitoring course content and standards. Finally the UL was a proper teaching university and was expanding accordingly. The UL moved to the Imperial Institute building in South Kensington to accommodate its expansion in 1900 and within twenty years, many of the colleges in London became schools under the umbrella of the UL including UCL.

Senate House – The Wanderer Returns to Bloomsbury – 1937

This monumental and iconic art deco tower boldly looks over Bloomsbury and Fitzrovia, and was the UL's way of declaring that they had returned – for good.

By the 1920s, the UL required larger premises and wanted its presence to be known as a permanent institution. By 1927, a large plot of land was purchased in Bloomsbury almost next to the UCL from the Duke of Bedford's Estate. The idea was that the new, permanent headquarters of the UL had to be bold and unique reflecting a new era, but also not imitate other universities. Senate House was built between 1933 and 1937 and was fully occupied by 1938. The building was designed by Charles Holden, the designer of many of London's underground stations. The imposing art deco Senate House finally put the UL on the world map.

The building is 210 feet (64 metres) high consisting of nineteen floors and was London's first skyscraper. The main building contains the UL's central academic bodies, the Senate House Library and administration offices.

Senate House under construction

Senate House was taken over by The Ministry of Information (MOI) during World War Two. The MOI was responsible for publicity and propaganda and is where the 'Keep Calm and Carry On' poster campaign was born.

George Orwell's novel, *Nineteen Eighty-Four* was inspired by Senate House where his wife worked during the war. Apparently, Orwell disliked the building but it provided him with the inspiration for 'The Ministry of Truth' in his 1948 dystopian novel. George Orwell died in 1950 of tuberculosis in University College Hospital at just 46 years old.

George Orwell, 1940

In 1969, Senate House was granted a Grade II* listed heritage site. Around Senate House is an array of UL schools and affiliated colleges such as the School of Oriental and African Studies (SOAS) and the London School of Hygiene and Tropical Medicine.

The Senate House building

The university's Bloomsbury quarter is only a proportion of the UL. Today, it owns 12 hectares of freehold land in Bloomsbury and some of the squares including Tavistock Square, Gordon Square, Torrington Square and Woburn Square. The UL also has colleges and institutes on their other estates across London as well as being a global university.

***

Notable former students include: Sir Frederick Gowland Hopkins who contributed greatly to the discovery of vitamins. He studied medicine and graduated in 1890 and was awarded the Nobel Prize in Physiology or Medicine in 1929. Sir Charles Kao who pioneered the use of fibre optics in telecommunications, gained a PhD in Electrical Engineering in 1956 and won a Nobel Prize in Physics 2009. Nelson Mandela, Anti-apartheid revolutionary who became President of South Africa from 1994 to 1999, studied law from prison during the 1960s and 1970s through a distance-learning programme but did not complete his degree. He was awarded the Nobel Peace Prize in 1993 that was shared with President Frederik Willem de Klerk (the man who had released him). Luisa Diogo, Prime Minister of Mozambique from 2004 to 2010, studied financial economics through online, blended and flexible learning and graduated in 1992.

The Almost Secret – Malet Street Gardens
(The Sunken Gardens)

Malet Street Gardens

In 1951, the UL purchased the rear gardens of a terraced row of houses on Gower Street, opposite Senate House to serve as a private garden. The terrace was built in 1780 for the Bedford Estate. One former resident, who lived at No. 2, was Dame Millicent Garrett Fawcett (1847–1929), a pioneer of women's suffrage and who played a major part in women obtaining the right to vote.

It is believed that the gardens are sunken due to the high-quality brick earth found here that was in high demand by local contractors. The garden is a small, leafy hidden gem and the entrance on Malet Street could be easily missed. The gardens are occasionally open to the public from April until September, weekdays, between eleven am and three pm.

The University College London (UCL)

University College London, Wilkins Building

As you approach the neo-Grecian style University College from Gower Street, one could be forgiven for thinking that you are entering an art gallery or museum. The chattering rows of students sitting on the steps, tucking into their snacks amongst the huge columns of the Wilkins Main Building reminds one that this is a place of learning. This happy and vibrant place is one of the world's leading universities.

This table briefly shows how UCL evolved. Note the subtle adjustments to its name to mark administrative changes.

Years	University College London (UCL)	Status
1836–1907	UCL Location: Gower Street (previously occupied by UL).	Affiliated to UL who awarded UCL students their degrees.
1907–1977	University of London, University College Location: Gower Street.	Merged with the UL losing its legal independence.
1977–2005	University College London Location: Gower Street.	In 1977, a new charter restored UCL's legal independence, although still powerless to award its own degrees until 2005.
2005–present	UCL Location: Gower Street (UCL Main Campus).	Granted its own degree awarding powers and re-branded itself as simply UCL. Became a global university.

Following the separation from UL in 1836 the freshly formed UCL started to grow and in 1842, the School of Pharmacy was founded. Upon the bequest from wealthy English art collector Felix Slade (1790–1868), who was a promoter of equality in education, the Slade School of Fine Art was founded in 1871.

In 1907, the UCL merged back with the UL and became a school of the UL. Gregory Foster became the UCL's first Principal in 1904 and relentlessly led the UCL to success during his term until 1929.

Foster quashed jealous rivalry between schools and departments, establishing many new departments that offered a wider range of study. The college physically expanded and student numbers trebled.

In 1937, the Institute of Archaeology was founded and is now one of the largest centres for archaeology in the world.

Second World War – The Great Hall Destroyed

During the Second World War, the UCL was seriously bombed and became Britain's hardest hit university. In 1940, the UCL's Great Hall was destroyed and the following year the main building and the dome were extensively damaged by fire from an air raid. The college's departments were relocated away from London. A steady rebuild, in Bloomsbury, started from 1945 and by 1954 the college was fully functioning again. Former student Stanley Joseph, who came to the UCL in 1947 and founded the UCL Film Society, described the college at the time as 'slightly unkempt and a bit of a shambles'.

Space, Science and Technology

There have been many scientific medical breakthroughs associated with the UCL. The elements krypton, neon and xenon were discovered at the UCL in 1898 by professor of chemistry William Ramsay who earned the nickname 'father of noble gases'. Ramsay would later be knighted in 1902 and receive the Nobel Prize in 1904. The DNA double helix was identified by former student, Francis Crick (UCL Physics, 1937) and James Watson in 1953.

During the 1960s the UCL was involved in the UK space programme at the Department of Space and Climate Physics that mainly operated outside of London. In 1973, the UCL's Institute for Computer Science became the first international link to the ARPANET (Advanced Research Projects Agency Network), the precursor of the internet. The UCL linked up with NORSAR (Norwegian Seismic Array), a research foundation in Norway.

Free at Last – 1977

In 1993, a reorganisation of the UL gave UCL direct access to government funding. The UCL received a new Royal Charter in 1977 that freed them from the UL's incorporation, allowing them to make independent decisions; however, they still relied upon the UL to award degrees until 2005 when the UCL was granted its own degree awarding powers. This boosted expansion and by 2005 the University College London rebranded itself simply as UCL.

***

As one will later discover, both the UL and UCL have a proud medical history, (see The Hospital and Medical Quarter – Gower Street area). The shiny new, £422 million University College Hospital on Euston Road was opened replacing the outdated original building. The Cancer Institute in the Paul O'Gorman Building in Huntley Street was opened in 2007. In 2016, the UCL was selected to be the operational headquarters of the UK Dementia Research Institute. The UCL has partners and associations with Great Ormond Street Hospital for Children and many more medical establishments at home and overseas.

***

Notable former students include: Alexander Graham Bell who was credited with the invention of the telephone studied phonics in 1868 but did not complete his studies. Gustav Holst, English composer known for his orchestral suite *The Planets,* studied languages and graduated in 1909. Junichiro Koizumi, Prime Minister of Japan from 2001 to 2006, graduated in economics in 1968. Christine Ohuruogu MBE, Olympian and athlete. At the 2008 Beijing Olympics she won a gold medal in the Women's 400 metres. She studied linguistics and graduated in 2005 and was awarded the Member of the Order of the British Empire (MBE) in 2009.

***

The UCL and UL are progressive, places of learning. As the UCL mentions on its website, it is elite but not elitist, and certainly has a friendly atmosphere. The UCL was ranked 10th in the world in the Quacquarelli Symonds World University Rankings (2019).

The Hospital and Medical Quarter – Gower Street Area

The Cruciform Building in front of The University College Hospital

The Cruciform Building in Gower Street, that was once the University College Hospital stands like a Victorian gothic castle contrasting against its more recent, pale turquoise replacement. The University College Hospital and UCL's main medical quarter occupies a large area from Gower Street to Tottenham Court Road and Euston Road to Torrington Place. Institutions such as the Macmillan Cancer Centre, the Hospital for Tropical Diseases and the Institute of Sport, Exercise and Health all lie within the area. This medical quarter of Bloomsbury has an interesting and significant history.

Medical Classes Began – 1828

Upon the opening of the London University in 1828, the first medical lecture was given by the anatomist, surgeon and physiologist

Charles Bell. This lecture marked the start of the university's medical classes and early school. During this time, many other medical classes were being taught in private schools owned and run by lecturers who often put profit before learners' needs. To remedy this unfair situation the university held lectures and had a temporary arrangement with the nearby Middlesex Hospital on Mortimer Street allowing students to observe medical practices.

The Dispensary Opens – 1828

Three days before the opening of the London University they opened their own dispensary on 28 September 1828, in a nearby house on Gower Street. It is believed the Dispensary had no beds, and was basically an outpatients and casualty department or clinic. Pharmaceutical training and post mortems were its main purpose. The Dispensary and the arrangements with the Middlesex Hospital continued until 1834 when the Dispensary closed and a new purpose-built North London Hospital opposite the university was opened in Gower Street.

The North London Hospital Opens – 1834

North London Hospital, Lithograph, 1834

There was a great need for a hospital in this area which was growing in population. The university launched an appeal in 1828 to raise funds to build a hospital to serve the sick and poor in the vicinity. The appeal offered certain rights and privileges to its donors. In 1833, it raised enough money to start construction of the new hospital on Gower Street opposite the London University and the first central block was opened in 1834. The hospital was the first of its kind in London to be built as a teaching hospital. Even before the hospital opened, student numbers had dramatically risen because of the courses on offer to them.

Upon the opening of the North London Hospital, surgeon Sir Robert Liston (1794–1847) was appointed to practice at the hospital and shortly afterwards he became professor of clinical surgery. Liston was often described as an arrogant showman and was known for the speed at which he performed surgery (very necessary to minimise pain during the pre-anaesthesia days).

London University in Gower Street became University College, London in 1836. In 1837, the North London Hospital was renamed University College Hospital. One of many medical achievements at the UCH took place in 1846 when Liston performed the first operation under anaesthetic in Europe.

A New University College Hospital (UCH) (Cruciform Building) – 1906

Cruciform Building

Despite many modifications and extensions, by 1877 it was decided that the hospital was too small and should be demolished and rebuilt. Student numbers and the needs of the ever-growing local population demanded a new hospital to be rebuilt on the same Gower Street site. Eighteen long, drawn-out years of planning commenced. During this time Dr George Vivian Poore, a physician working at the hospital, suggested that the new building should take the shape of a cruciform. The idea being that a cross shape would help improve ventilation, drainage and lighting. In the meantime, it was business as usual; however, the hospital was becoming overcrowded and chaotic.

The architect Alfred Waterhouse (1830–1905) came up with two designs for the new hospital: one was the cruciform suggestion from Dr Poore and the second, a more conventional quadrangular form. Dr Poore's cruciform was chosen despite it requiring a little more land. A rebuilding fund was already well underway raising money from successful ex-students, and wealthy donations and bequests. In 1896, Sir John Blundell Maple, a wealthy entrepreneur who owned the Tottenham Court Road furniture maker Maple & Co, was overwhelmed with Waterhouse's plans. Maple took it upon himself to fund the project including new medical equipment at a cost of £100,000.

Twenty-nine years after the initial decision was made the new hospital was finally officially opened in 1906. Sadly, Alfred Waterhouse died before the hospital's official opening.

Built in the shape of St Andrew's cross the new hospital that was also known as the cruciform building was met with admiration for its clean and airy design and good use of space. At this time, the 1905 UCL Transfer Act led to the separation of the medical school and UCH in 1907. The separation of the hospital relieved the UCL of some of its financial burden. Clinical teaching ceased at the college and continued at the hospital while the preclinical school remained. The hospital was steadily going from strength to strength drawing attention to its own success. The development of a medical quarter at the UCL started in 1909 with the building of the Institute of Physiology, which was followed in 1912 by pharmacology thanks to a very large donation by Industrialist Andrew Carnegie.

The Rockefeller Foundation's Big Gift

Founded in America in 1913 by the Rockefeller family, The Rockefeller Foundation set out with the mission of 'promoting the well-being of humanity throughout the world'. Two representatives visiting London in 1919 were impressed with new surgical units being started and the college's and hospital's advancements in medical education. The following year, the hospital, medical school and college received a huge grant. Thanks to the Rockefeller gift a building programme started with a new obstetric hospital almost next door in Huntley Street and a new nurses' home. The main hospital was reorganised and improved. A new Radiological Department for diagnosis and therapy, and Skin and Orthopaedic Departments were established. New departments and facilities continued growing in and around the immediate vicinity such as the Anatomy Building that opened in 1923. The college, medical school and hospital had formed a medical quarter in Bloomsbury that today is world class.

Second World War

When the Second World War broke out the UCH, under the Ministry of Health's Emergency Hospital Scheme, became a casualty clearing station. All non-critical patients were sent home or to hospitals outside of London. Vulnerable areas around the hospital were shielded by walls of sandbags. The hospital never received a direct hit from the air raids, but equipment was damaged caused by vibrations as bombs hit the surrounding area. The UCL, however, received significant bomb damage that took many years after the war to rebuild and return to normality.

The National Health Service – 1948 Onwards

Upon the establishment of the National Health Service (NHS) in 1948 the hospital was designated a teaching hospital with the medical school becoming independent from UCL. The same year St Pancras Hospital and the Hospital for Tropical Diseases were incorporated into the UCH.

The 1950s saw the hospital's facilities improve vastly. In 1951, the Metabolic and Isotope Wards and a Premature Baby Unit opened. By 1954, many patients enjoyed wards that had beds with curtains and over-bed Formica tables with three-way radio and a bedside locker. Food was kept warm during the journey from the main kitchen using electrically heated trolleys. Apparently, the food was good and patients could enjoy a smoke any time except during ward rounds.

By the early 1960s, the hospital had over 500 beds and good accommodation for staff and continued to expand its range of treatments.

The 1960s and 1970s was business as usual despite the NHS starting its reorganisation of management from 1974. In 1982, as a result of the reorganisation, the UCH and the Middlesex Hospital became united under the administration of Bloomsbury District Health Authority. The University College London Hospitals NHS Trust followed in 1994 and incorporated the UCH, the Middlesex Hospital (that closed in 2005), and many more.

The old cruciform building closed as a hospital in 1995 and was purchased by the UCL and officially named the Cruciform Building. Today, the occupants in the building include: Wolfson Institute for Biomedical Research, Division of Infection and Immunity, Intensive Care Medicine, UK Dementia Research Institute and the Cruciform Hub which contains a library, teaching and study areas. The UCL is recognised as a world leader in medical education.

Baroque-style interior: Cruciform Building

The Cruciform Building with its imposing exterior and slightly flamboyant baroque-style interior has stood the test of time. Staff and guests are privileged to admire its ornate interior beauty. Stand outside the Gower Street or Huntley Street sides and one will see the new and old hospitals in photogenic unison.

One may also see the ghost of Lizzie Church, a trainee nurse who, in the 1890s, accidentally gave her fiancé (who was a patient at the time) a fatal dose of morphine. Riddled with guilt Lizzie committed suicide only to reappear: patients and staff claim to have seen her ghost; keeping an eye on patients about to receive injections, to avoid the same mistake happening again.

The New University College Hospital – 2005

The new University College Hospital

A new state of the art hospital was built behind the original site, located just slightly to the north on Euston Road, close to Warren Street and Euston Square tube stations. The Queen opened the new light and airy UCH building in 2005, which is still a research and learning hospital associated with the UCL.

NORTH CENTRAL

Church of Christ the King from Gordon Square and Gardens

Putting aside the allure of the universities, this area also offers many of Bloomsbury's well-loved attractions including its famous squares, which gave the world some of its greatest writers, artists and thinkers, a mini Westminster Abbey and many free first-class museums.

Wellcome Collection – Euston Road

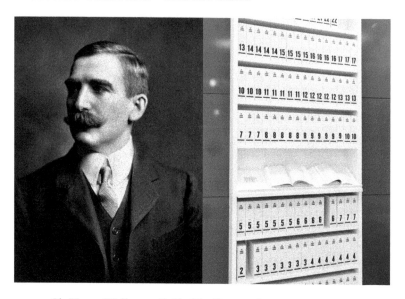

Sir Henry Wellcome (left). The Human Genome Bookcase, Wellcome Collection *Medicine Now*

At Bloomsbury's northern boundary on Euston Road is a fascinating, spacious museum dedicated to medicine, science, art and life, and to quote their literature, 'the incurably curious'. The Wellcome empire runs along Euston Road stretching from Gower Street to Gordon Street. The Wellcome Trust Headquarters building that was opened in 2004, complements the UCH adjacent. The glass and steel headquarters are linked to its 1930s Wellcome Building that houses the famous collection and library.

Wellcome is a global charitable foundation supporting new ideas in the sciences. The Wellcome Collection exhibits a mixture of medical antiquities, artefacts and artwork. The collection also has modern hi-tech displays and artworks. Founded in 2007, the collection is part of the Wellcome Trust charity that was founded in 1936 by the bequest of pharmacist, entrepreneur and collector Sir Henry Solomon Wellcome (1853–1936).

In 1880, American born Henry and his college friend Silas Burroughs established the pharmaceutical company Burroughs Wellcome & Co that became a multinational enterprise. Burroughs died in 1895 leaving Henry solely in charge. The Wellcome enterprise funded important research. Henry's first invention was invisible ink, made from lemon juice when he was 16 years old.

Sir Henry collected a vast array of books, paintings and objects relating to the historical development of medicine which are now located in the original Wellcome Building; there is also a library, reading room and a hub for researchers to meet. Admission to the collection and exhibitions is free. The building is very large and one may spend more time there than planned as one discovers its wealth of exhibits.

Tavistock Square and Gardens

Sculpture of Mahatma Gandhi in Tavistock Square Gardens

After arriving at Euston or St Pancras stations, negotiating Euston Road's often gridlocked traffic, one enters Bloomsbury's Upper Woburn Place, where many travellers embrace this calm oasis. Here, one can take stock before joining the parade of people arriving at their hotels and wheeling their luggage behind them.

In the 1700s, Tavistock Square was open marshy fields where locals hunted ducks and illegal duelling took place. Tavistock Square's name originates from Francis Russell, Marquess of Tavistock the eldest son of John Russell, 4th Duke of Bedford. James Burton built the east side of the square in around 1803 for John Russell, 6th Duke of Bedford who owned the land. During the 1820s, master builder Thomas Cubitt (1788–1855) continued to develop Tavistock Square and completed it by around 1826.

Between 1851 and 1860, Charles Dickens lived in Tavistock House at the northern side of the square. Here he wrote classics such as *Bleak House* (1853), *Hard Times* (1854), *Little Dorrit* (published in instalments between 1855 and 1857) and *A Tale of Two Cities* (1859). Tavistock House was another fine example of James Burton's work, but was demolished in 1901 and the new building is now the headquarters of the British Medical Association.

In 1967, a cherry tree was planted in the gardens as a memorial to the victims of the of Hiroshima and Nagasaki atomic bombings. The centrepiece of the gardens is a sculpture of Mahatma Gandhi by Fredda Brilliant, a Polish sculptor and actress. The statue was installed in 1968. The Conscientious Objectors Commemorative Stone was added to the gardens by the Peace Pledge Union in 1994 to commemorate objectors worldwide. To many the square is regarded as a centre of peace and holds annual ceremonies at each of these memorials.

In the gardens, a bust of Virginia Woolf was unveiled in 2004. Woolf and her husband Leonard resided at 52 Tavistock Square between 1924 and 1939 (now the Tavistock Hotel). The Woolfs moved their famous Hogarth Press from Richmond upon Thames to No. 52 and published a large variety of works for notable authors such as John Maynard Keynes' *The end of laissez-faire* (1926) and William Plomer's *Paper Houses* (1929). In 1940, Tavistock Square and the Woolf's home and business were devastated by a bomb during the Blitz.

Tragically, a double-decker bus in Tavistock Square fell victim to the London terrorist bombings of 2005, killing thirteen people around the British Medical Association headquarters. The 7/7 Tavistock Square Memorial Trust have placed a memorial plaque within the gardens opposite the British Medical Association. In total, fifty-two people died across London on that tragic day.

Gordon Square and Gardens

Gordon Square and Gardens

Within these gardens one can sit on a bench and take in the vibrant atmosphere, watching students meet up and people sprawled out on the grass appearing not to have a care in the world. Situated in the university quarter, and with its association with the Bloomsbury Group, this square is definitely a place for reflection. The well-kept gardens, lined with mature trees and well-kept shrubs, certainly give one the opportunity to think clearly.

As one of a pair with Tavistock Square (a block away), Gordon Square Gardens were designed by John Russell, 6th Duke of Bedford in 1820. Gordon Square is named after the duke's second wife, Lady Georgiana Gordon. Like Tavistock Square, Gordon Square was also developed by Thomas Cubitt from the 1820s onward. Thomas Cubitt was known for his Greek revival and Italianate styles that are noticeable in Gordon Square's houses, especially on the west side. The formal Georgian-style houses on the east and west sides of the gardens were completed by 1850.

***

In the early twentieth century, the houses around the square became the focal point of the Bloomsbury Group: John Maynard Keynes lived at 46 Gordon Square from 1916 until 1946; earlier the same house was occupied by Virginia Woolf from 1904 until 1907. Prominent member of the Bloomsbury Group Lytton Strachey lived at No. 51 from 1921 until his death in 1932. The School of Arts, Birkbeck, UL now occupy Nos. 43–46. Currently, the square is owned and maintained by the UL and is open to the public.

Gordon Square, a focal point of the Bloomsbury Group

Leading on to the south of Gordon Square Gardens is Woburn Square Gardens that takes one to the UL's School of Oriental and African Studies and Birkbeck. The rather plain and disappointing building to the north of Gordon Square Gardens is the UCL Institute of Archaeology. Heading north up Gordon Street from Gordon Square is the innovative and charming Bloomsbury Theatre and Studio that is owned by the UCL.

Around Gordon Square and Byng Place

With its three red telephone boxes, Byng Place (opposite the UL) offers some seating and light refreshments. Here one can look over to the UL and watch students making haste to get to their lectures on time! Every Thursday from nine am until two pm there is a farmer's market in Torrington Square directly opposite the church.

The Church of Christ the King

The Church of Christ the King

A Grade I listed building since 1954, this impressive Gothic Revival masterpiece and 'mini Westminster Abbey' immediately grabs one's attention. In the early 1840s Gordon Square was not complete, and the Bedford Estates broke its policy of residential buildings only. The Church of Christ the King was built between 1851 and 1854 for the Catholic Apostolic Church by British architect and architectural writer John Raphael Rodrigues Brandon (1817–77).

The church never reached its intended grandeur which would have included a 300 feet spire. The congregation were often mistakenly referred to as 'Irvingites' after the controversial minister Edward Irving (1792–1834) who had died before the Catholic Apostolic Church had been formed. From 1963, the UL's Anglican Chaplaincy took over the church which became known as University Church of Christ the King until 1994. Today, the church building is used by two organisations: Euston Church and Forward in Faith.

In 2015, the trustees of the Church of Christ the King offered the use of their building to Euston Church who are an evangelical church. Euston Church holds Sunday services and mid-week meetings. The entrance is in Byng Place.

The English Chapel within the church is used by the Catholic organisation, Forward in Faith for weekday services. In 1992, Forward in Faith leased the English Chapel from the trustees of the Catholic Apostolic Church. Forward in Faith is a traditionalist strand within the Anglican Church that is opposed to the ordination of women to the priesthood.

The Petrie Museum of Egyptian Archaeology – Malet Place

Statuette of an Egyptian man and his wife, 18th Dynasty:
The Petrie Museum of Egyptian Archaeology

Tucked away in Malet Place is this UCL-owned museum that is free to enter. The small museum contains an estimated 80,000 Egyptian and Sudanese archaeological objects depicting life in the Nile Valley from predynastic (before recorded history) Egypt and Sudan, to the Islamic period (AD 642 to present day). This university museum was set up as a teaching resource for the Department of Egyptian Archaeology and Philology at the UCL in 1892. The museum was established thanks to the bequest of the writer, adventurer and explorer Amelia Edwards (1831–92), who donated her collection of important Egyptian artefacts. Later the collection grew significantly in size and fame mainly thanks to the remarkable excavating career and contributions made by Egyptologist and archaeologist William Flinders Petrie (1853–1942). In 1915, the Petrie Museum of Egyptian Archaeology opened to visitors and, dare I say, the rest is history.

The Grant Museum of Zoology – University Street

This is a small and, sometimes, crowded natural history museum located on the corner of University Street and Gower Street in the UCL's Rockefeller Building. Entrance is free and well worth a visit. This quirky museum is packed with the weird and wonderful. One will find more than 68,000 zoological specimens, objects and curiosities. The exhibits include a rare quagga skeleton, dodo bones, material from the Discovery and Challenger expeditions as well as items from London Zoo. It is one of the oldest collections of natural history in the UK. The Grant Museum of Zoology was established in 1827 by Professor of Comparative Anatomy, Robert Edmond Grant (1793–1874). The museum was set up as a teaching collection of zoological specimens and opened to the public in 1996. The museum is part of UCL and has been used by students since it was established.

SOUTH CENTRAL

Russell Square: Statue of Francis Russell, 5th Duke of Bedford

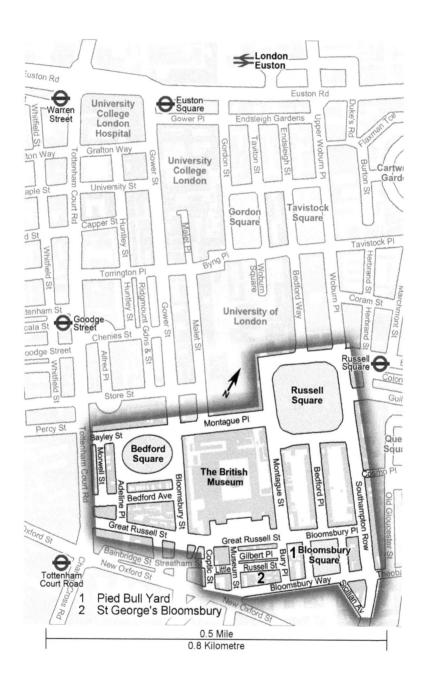

London Euston
Euston Rd
Euston Rd
Warren Street
University College London Hospital
Euston Square
Gower Pl
Endsleigh Gardens
Endsleigh St
Upper Woburn Pl
Duke's Rd
Flaxman Tce
Whitfield St
ton Way
Grafton Way
Tottenham Court Rd
Gower St
University College London
Gordon St
Taviton St
Burton St
Cartwr Gard
aple St
University St
Capper St
Huntley St
Maple Pl
Gordon Square
Tavistock Square
d St
Whitfield St
Torrington Pl
Byng Pl
Woburn Square
Tavistock Pl
Herbrand St
Coram St
Marchmont St
tenham St
cala St
Goodge Street
Huntley St
Ridgmount Gdns & St
Gower St
Malet St
Woburn Square
Bedford Way
Woburn Pl
Herbrand St
oodge Street
Chenies St
Alfred Pl
University of London
Russell Square
Colon
Whitfield St
Store St
Russell Square
Guil
Percy St
Montague Pl
Que Squ
Bayley St
Tottenham Court Rd
Morwell St
Bedford Square
Bloomsbury St
The British Museum
Montague St
Bedford Pl
Southampton Row
Cosmo Pl
Old Gloucester St
Adeline Pl
Bedford Ave
Great Russell St
Great Russell St
Bloomsbury Pl
Oxford St
Bainbridge St
New Oxford St
Streatham St
Coptic St
Museum St
Little
Russell St
Gilbert Pl
Bury Pl
1 Bloomsbury Square
2
Bloomsbury Way
Sicilian Av
Theoba
Tottenham Court Road
Charing Cross Rd
New Oxford St

1   Pied Bull Yard
2   St George's Bloomsbury

0.5 Mile
0.8 Kilometre

One can clearly understand why this is the most popular and visited part of Bloomsbury. Tourists hastily aim straight for The British Museum and fit in a bit of souvenir shopping before moving on to tick off other London *must see* destinations. Visitors, who are lucky enough to have more time on their side, will soon discover the south's rich offerings.

Bedford Square and Gardens

Bedford Square and Gardens

To say Bedford Square is unspoilt is an understatement, it is exactly how one might imagine a London Georgian square to be. Symmetric and elegantly uniformed Georgian terraces line the square reflecting the square's rich past, though many of these splendid former homes are now almost disguised as offices. Today the square is known as one of the finest and most well-preserved squares in London. Houses 1–54 are listed Grade I on the Historic England Register.

The 4th Duke of Bedford planned the square that was eventually built between 1775 and 1783 by the 4th duke's widow, Gertrude Leveson-Gower. Architect Thomas Leverton (1743–1824) is believed to have been mainly involved in the design of Bedford Square along with builders William Scott and Robert Grews. Leverton designed some of the square's interiors including his own at No. 13, where he died in 1824.

***

The square has had many well-known occupants including: John Scott, first Earl of Eldon and Lord Chancellor from 1801 to 1806 and again from 1807 to 1827, who resided at No. 6; pioneering engine designer Sir Harry Ricardo (1885–1974) was born and lived at No. 13.

Bloomsbury Publishing Plc's head office is situated at No. 50. This highly successful British independent publishing house was founded in 1986 by Nigel Newton. The company's success is due to publications such as the *Harry Potter* series by J. K. Rowling and its highly acclaimed academic and professional publishing division. They have offices worldwide.

***

Many garden squares in London's past were only accessible to the residents. Staying true to this tradition Bedford Square Gardens is not normally open to the public but can be visited during Open Garden Squares Weekend. Many of London's private square gardens open their gates to the public in early June for one weekend.

Russell Square and Gardens

Russell Square and Gardens

Surrounded by the continuous flow of traffic, Russell Square is one of London's biggest squares; however, the gardens are surprisingly relaxing and offer a shady retreat in summer. Here one can watch the world go by as students and tourists cross the park to get to their destinations, or be amused by squirrels foraging for food. Within the gardens is a pleasant Anglo-Italian café with terraces and a rather calming water fountain. Some of the Georgian buildings that surround the square are simply façades with the internal walls knocked through to create more functional office space. On the west side around Senate House Library the buildings are pseudo-Georgian. Nevertheless the square still retains some of its original aristocratic charm.

Thomas Wriothesley (1505–50), 1st Earl of Southampton and Chancellor of England, was granted the Manor of Bloomsbury by Henry VIII in 1545. In 1657, Wriothesley's great-grandson, who was also named Thomas Wriothesley (1608–67), the 4th Earl of

Southampton started to develop the area and built Southampton House in 1657. The house was later renamed Bedford House after 1734 when it came into the ownership of the Dukes of Bedford and sat on today's Bedford Place that links Russell Square to Bloomsbury Square.

When the 4th Earl of Southampton died in 1667 he left the Bloomsbury Estate to his daughter, Lady Rachel Vaughan (1636–1723) who, in 1669, married William, Lord Russell (1639–83). William was the son and heir of the 5th Earl of Bedford and this marriage brought the Bloomsbury Estate into the Russell family which holds the peerage title of Duke of Bedford. In 1683, William, Lord Russell was accused of taking part in the Rye House Plot to murder King Charles II and his Catholic brother James, Duke of York. He was found guilty of treason and beheaded at Lincoln's Inn Fields. Over the following years the Russell family, managed the steady development of their estate. By 1775, the construction of Bedford Square had started and the development of suburban upper-middle-class northern Bloomsbury began.

Francis Russell, 5th Duke of Bedford (1765–1802), was a gambler and big spender. During his short life the duke sold parts of Bloomsbury for development. The result of which can be seen at Russell Square, Montague Street, Bedford Place and Tavistock Square (completed by his brother John Russell, 6th Duke of Bedford). Francis was not impressed with his mansion, Bedford House (previously named Southampton House). Francis preferred the upmarket and glamorous West End that had excellent development potential. In 1800, he auctioned off the contents of Bedford House before having it demolished.

Francis Russell instructed developer James Burton to build a development of terraced houses that included the south and west part of Russell Square, as well as the north part of Bloomsbury Square and Bedford Place. The landscaping of both garden squares was part of the agreement. Burton designated English landscape designer Humphry Repton (1752–1818) to design and create a visual link between the squares. Humphry Repton completed this link by placing two statues in each direction (both bronze statues by the sculptor Sir Richard Westmacott RA).

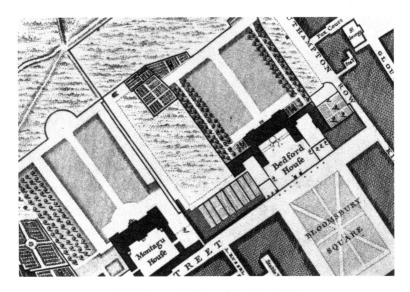

John Rocque's Map of London, 1746

After the demolition of Bedford House work began around 1804 and was completed in 1806. The unmarried Duke of Bedford died before the completion of his vision in 1802. His brother inherited the title of John Russell, 6th Duke of Bedford, who was the father of Liberal Prime Minister John Russell, 1st Earl Russell (Prime Minister from 1846 to 1852 and 1865 to 1866).

At the entrance to Russell Square, an information board has the following description: 'The bronze statue by Sir Richard Westmacott RA was unveiled on 3rd August 1809. It depicts Sir Francis Russell, the agriculturalist (a member of the first Board of Agriculture), with his hand on a plough, sheep at his feet and four cherubs representing spring, summer, autumn and winter.' This statue looks out of the square on to Bedford Place. At the north end of Bloomsbury Square is the second statue by Westmacott that was erected in 1816. This statue depicts the duke's political hero Charles James Fox (1749– 1806), a politician and opponent of the slave trade; in his right hand he holds the Magna Carta looking down Bedford Place back towards Sir Francis Russell's statue in Russell Square.

Russell Square was restored back to many of its original features in 2002. The restoration included lime trees and a path layout complete with new railings and gates. The original iron work was removed and recycled as part of the World War Two war effort. Russell Square is still owned by the Bedford Estates whose offices are situated on the south end of Montague Street. Russell Square and Bloomsbury Square are maintained by Camden Council and they are open to the public during daylight hours.

Around Russell Square

As I have mentioned, the square has undergone some changes over time with large parts of the eastern side making way for hotels during the latter part of the nineteenth century and the UL's developments in the twentieth century. New and old coexist quite well, and around the square there are some interesting mixes of architectural styles.

The Principal London Hotel

The Principal London Hotel

In Russell Square one will certainly notice a huge Victorian monster of a hotel, called The Principal London and which was formerly known as the Hotel Russell. Prior to the hotel being built, women's rights campaigner Emmeline Pankhurst (1858–1928) and husband Dr Richard Pankhurst lived here with their family at 8 Russell Square from 1888 to 1893.

The hotel was designed by the architect Charles Fitzroy Doll (1850–1929) and opened in 1898. The building is a masterpiece clad in terracotta thé-au-lait (tea with milk) decorative style and was based on the sixteenth-century Château de Madrid in Paris. The elaborate designs decorate all eight storeys! Life-size statues by architectural sculptor Henry Charles Fehr (1867–1940) of four queens: Elizabeth, Mary, Anne, and Victoria stand above the hotel's main entrance.

The striking attention to detail and the extravagant exterior, which glows a beautiful salmon pink in certain light, is enough to take one aback. The hotel is equally as impressive inside with its palatial marble claddings in a variety of colours. One will not be surprised to learn that the hotel is Grade II* listed. Remember that it will be more than probable to find oneself viewing this magnificent architecture from the very busy Russell Square's Southampton Row rather than any other perspective, so watch the traffic.

Imperial Hotel

Next to The Principal London hotel on the other side of Guilford Street are The President and Imperial hotels, both built in the mid-twentieth century, yet do not share the same grandeur as The Principal. The original Imperial Hotel that was built between 1905 and 1911 stood on the same site as the current Imperial Hotel.

Imperial Hotel early 1900s

The first hotel was also designed by Charles Fitzroy Doll. This massive building was equally, if not more, extravagant as its neighbouring Hotel Russell. The original Imperial Hotel was a combination of Art Nouveau Gothic and Tudor style architecture. The Greater London Council ordered the demolition of the Imperial Hotel in 1966 claiming 'the whole frame was so structurally unsound that there was no possibility of saving it if a preservation order had been placed on the building'.

Cabmen's Shelters

Cabmen's Shelter: Russell Square

At the north-west corner of Russell Square, just outside the park, is a green hut dressed with potted plants hanging from its exterior. This charming garden-shed-looking structure once served as a shelter for horse-drawn taxi drivers. The hut is no bigger than a horse and cart and has a chimney that once served the wood-burning stove inside. It is a fully functioning café where one can get a cup of coffee, however, only London taxi drivers are permitted inside. London has thirteen Cabmen's Shelters remaining and all are Grade II listed.

The story goes, that one snowy day in January 1875, George Armstrong, editor of the Fleet Street newspaper *The Globe*, sent his servant to get a cab to Fleet Street. The servant reported back, informing Armstrong that all the cabbies were taking shelter and drinking in the pub. He shared his concerns with others, including the Earl of Shaftesbury, and that same year the Cabmen's Shelters fund was established for hansom cabs. Thanks to the fund, Cabmen could conveniently rest, eat and drink in their own dwelling and at affordable prices.

The Wiener Library

On the western side of Russell Square in a smart period terrace house at No. 29, is a library dedicated to the study of the Holocaust and genocide. The archives on the Holocaust and Nazi era are one of the world's leading collections. The ever-growing collection has over one million items that include press cuttings, eyewitness testimonies and photographs, and the Library also holds many exhibitions and events.

The Wiener Library started its story in the 1920s when Dr Alfred Wiener, a German Jew who fought in World War One, returned to Germany in 1919. He was horrified at the rise of anti-Semitism and decided to work with the Central Association of German Citizens of Jewish Faith. In 1925, he gathered information about the Nazi Party to help undermine them (the same year Hitler published *Mein Kampf*).

In 1933, Wiener and his family fled Germany and settled in Amsterdam where he set up the Jewish Central Information Office

(JCIO) and continued to add to his archives. Following the November anti-Jewish pogroms of 1938, Wiener prepared his collection to be sent to Britain and reopened the JCIO in London's Marylebone. It is believed that his collection was opened on 1 September 1939, the day the Nazis invaded Poland.

The information gathered by the JCIO served the British Government well during the war and was referred to as 'Dr Wiener's Library'. After the war the library proved a vital asset in aiding prosecutors at the Nuremberg Trials between 1945 and 1946. Eventually his collection helped to shape the academic study of the Holocaust.

In 2011, The Wiener Library moved to Russell Square and, with help from the Heritage Lottery Fund, they made improvements to attract a wider audience. The Wiener Library is informative, thought provoking and a sad reminder of what humanity is capable of doing to itself.

Bloomsbury Square and Gardens

Bloomsbury Square and Gardens

With busy Bloomsbury Way at the south perimeter and Great Russell Street (Bloomsbury Square) to the north, one would not be surprised to learn that this garden square is not quite as relaxing as some of Bloomsbury's green spaces. However, despite being in a busy location, the square is a good place to plan one's onward travels (Covent Garden is about half a mile away).

The square was originally called Southampton Square, and it is believed to be the earliest named square in London. It was laid out in the early 1660s by the 4th Earl of Southampton, Thomas Wriothesley, as the piazza for his mansion, Southampton House.

Redevelopment started in 1800 when Francis, 5th Duke of Bedford, demolished Bedford House. By 1814, James Burton had completed the Georgian terraced houses on the north side of Bloomsbury Square. Bedford Place was built and at the same time Humphry Repton redesigned Bloomsbury Square (see Russell Square and Gardens).

Around Bloomsbury Square

Victoria House

Victoria House

On the east side one will, without question, notice the stunning 1920s neoclassical Greek-inspired Victoria House that occupies the entire eastern side of the square. The building was designed by Charles William Long for the insurance and investment company, Liverpool Victoria Friendly Society. The company acquired the land from the Duke of Bedford in 1920; however, for a short time, the existing leaseholders were unwilling to vacate their premises. Due to this inconvenience, builders had to start construction at each end, eventually meeting up in the middle on the Southampton Row side. The northern end was completed in 1926 and by 1932, the entire building was officially opened. Victoria House had become the largest office block in the country apart from Whitehall. The building certainly lives up to its original specification which was to 'add to the dignity and beauty of the metropolis'.

During World War Two the basements were converted into air raid shelters. The building also accommodated first aid and gas-decontamination stations and police and fire brigade sub-stations.

Liverpool Victoria Friendly Society (known today as LV=) relocated to Bournemouth in 1996 and the building was shortlisted to become London's city hall. However, this did not come to pass and the following year it was purchased by Garbe UK. The building was sympathetically remodelled shortly afterwards. Today, Victoria House is a highly sought after mixed-use building with apartments, offices and retail businesses. This magnificent house still has its grand original art deco ballroom that is currently used by the famous London Cabaret Club. The building is a Grade II listed landmark of Bloomsbury Square and Southampton Row.

***

Notable former residents of the square include: the benefactor of The British Museum, Sir Hans Sloane who lived at Nos. 3–4 Bloomsbury Place from 1695 to 1742; the founder of English dermatology Dr Robert Willan (1757–1812) who lived at Nos. 9–11 Bloomsbury Square. Benjamin Disraeli (1804–81), who was

Conservative Party leader and twice Prime Minister lived at No. 6 between 1817 and 1824 from the age of thirteen. The large house also has an ornate white plaque dedicated to his father, Isaac, who was a highly successful author.

Sicilian Avenue

Sicilian Avenue

This quirky, mini Italian-style treasure is a little out of keeping with its surrounding area. One cannot help but look up and admire the intricate architecture and bayed window turrets. Sicilian Avenue was designed by architect Robert Worley (1850–1930) and was built between 1906 and 1910 and is believed to be the first purpose-built pedestrianised street in London.

Sicilian Avenue is a Grade II listed pedestrian cut-through from Bloomsbury Way and Vernon Place to Southampton Row. At each end of the avenue, one is greeted by grand columned entranceways supporting balustrades on top with gold lettering spelling out the name Sicilian Avenue. From the Southampton Row entrance there are two tall, coned roof turrets. This very stylish shortcut is said to be paved in Sicilian stone and is lined with al fresco restaurants and a few shops.

The Holborn Whippet

This public house is on the Bloomsbury end of the avenue and specialises in beer from small craft breweries, and serves quality wines and food.

Great Russell Street

Great Russell Street

With tourists marching towards The British Museum, obstructing the way as they stop to take selfies or compose that perfect photograph of the museum, souvenir shops offering toy buses and replica Big Bens and the Museum Tavern all make up busy Great Russell Street. In the vicinity are some fine hotels, pubs and the obligatory souvenir shops.

Great Russell Street runs from Tottenham Court Road eastwards to Bloomsbury Square and is the tourist route to The British Museum and throughway to Southampton Row. Great Russell Street is not as the name suggests, it is a narrow two-lane street.

Down some of the side streets one can have a cheap breakfast or a pint (The Plough in Little Russell Street for example) or browse the small shops. The Camera Museum, in Museum Street is a second-hand camera shop and café with its own free museum and gallery.

Named after the Russell family, Great Russell Street was developed from around 1670 onwards. The street followed an old rural path called Green Lane. By 1679, Montagu House had been built on Great Russell Street and by 1720 most of the street had been developed into houses. By the mid-1800s, Bedford Estates redeveloped the south side of the street.

Historian and biographer John Strype (1643–1737) in his 1720 *Survey of London* described the street as, 'a very handsome large and well-built Street, graced with the best Buildings, and the best inhabited by the Nobility and Gentry, especially the North side, as having Gardens behind the Houses and the Prospect of the pleasant Fields up to Hamsted and Highgate. Insomuch that this Place by Physicians is esteemed the most healthful of any in London'.

***

Great Russell Street saw its fair share of artisans, academics and professionals come and go: portrait painter John Philip Davis ('Pope' Davis) died at No. 67 in 1862 and artist, novelist George du

Maurier lived at No. 91 in 1863 until 1868. Architect John Nash (1752–1835) started his career in Great Russell Street when he completed his first works at Nos. 67–70.

The British Museum

The British Museum

The approach to the south entrance and forecourt from Great Russell Street is spectacular. The huge iron railing with two relatively small open gates, reveals the museum's Greek revival architecture that beckons one into one of the world's finest museums.

Montagu House Where The British Museum Started

The British Museum in Montagu House

Ralph Montagu, 1st Duke of Montagu (1638–1709) built Montagu House between 1677 and 1679 to the designs of scientist and architect Robert Hooke (1635–1703). This magnificent and elaborate French-style mansion was briefly occupied by the Dukes of Montagu. The house was severely damaged by a fire in 1686 and rebuilt soon after by the French architect Pierre Puget (1620–94).

The Mad Duchess of Albemarle

Within two years of his first wife's death, Ralph Montagu married Lady Elizabeth Monck, Duchess of Albemarle in 1692. Elizabeth had a history of mental illness and was often reported as not being aware of her actions. She had inherited a fortune from her first husband who died aged 35 in 1688. Elizabeth declared that she would not marry again unless to a reigning monarch. Ralph spent his entire courtship with Elizabeth dressed as the Emperor of China, and won her hand in marriage, and a fortune. Once married, and living in Montagu House, Elizabeth believed she was the Empress of China. The few guests that Ralph allowed to visit Elizabeth entertained her delusion with amusement. After the death of Ralph Montagu in 1709 his son John, 2nd Duke of Montagu accumulated large debts and abandoned Montagu House in 1731 and moved to a smaller Montagu House in Whitehall. Montagu House in Bloomsbury stood empty and neglected until the Montagu family sold it in 1755.

The Beginning of The British Museum

The physician, naturalist and collector, Sir Hans Sloane (1660–1753) upon his death bequeathed his lifetime collection of over 71,000 objects to King George II for the nation in return for a £20,000 payment to his heirs. The collection was purchased and in 1753 Parliament established The British Museum. Sloane's vast collections consisted of books, manuscripts, natural specimens and some antiquities. Later, in 1757, King George gave the new museum a collection of manuscripts collected by English sovereigns from Edward IV onwards, referred to now as the Old Royal Library.

The newly established British Museum purchased the abandoned Montagu House in 1755, and Montagu House gardens were opened to the public in 1757. Later in 1759, after refurbishments had been completed, the public were allowed inside Montagu House to view the museum's collections. The museum welcomed 'all studious and curious Persons' with free entry as it continues to do to this day. During the 1800s, the museum saw important acquisitions, the most commonly known is the Rosetta Stone in 1802.

Montagu House had refurbishments and additions made in order to accommodate the ever increasing collections but the house was ultimately too small. Three sides of a quadrangle, designed by the distinguished architect Sir Robert Smirke (1780–1867), were constructed to the north of Montagu House, and subsequently the house was demolished in 1845, making way for a larger British Museum. The quadrangular building designed by Smirke in 1823 was complete by 1852.

In 1851, the museum appointed Sir Augustus Wollaston Franks (1826–97) as assistant in the Department of Antiquities. Later he was the museum's first Keeper of British and Medieval Antiquities and Ethnography. Franks broadened the museum's collections and, with his creative thinking and personal contributions, vastly increased the museum's popularity.

The round Reading Room, the centrepiece of the Great Court, was designed by the younger brother of Sir Robert Smirke, Sydney Smirke (1798–1877) and completed in 1857. The Reading Room instantly became a great London sight and a reputable place of learning. Famous reading pass holders included Vladimir Lenin and Karl Marx, to mention a few. In 1997, the Reading Room's books were moved to the new British Library in Euston Road that officially opened in 1998.

Built in the space vacated by the library, The Queen Elizabeth II Great Court was completed and opened to the public in 2000. Designed by Foster and Partners, the courtyard is the largest covered public space in Europe, sheltering two-acres under its beautiful glass roof with the famous Reading Room proudly sitting in the centre.

The British Museum: The Queen Elizabeth II Great Court

History of Montague Street

Montague Street

This street was named after the owner of Montagu House, Ralph Montagu and runs from Russell Square south-eastward to Great Russell Street. This is a smart and uniformed formal street that has a steady flow of tourists checking into its hotels or making their way to The British Museum just around the corner.

Montague Street was mainly developed to the designs of James Burton by the builder W. E. Allen between 1803 and 1806. The street was originally the boundary line between Montagu House and Bedford House. Today, Montague Street with its neat, large stuccoed houses with iron balconies on their first floors, is mainly occupied by small stylish hotels and businesses.

***

Writer Arthur Conan Doyle (1859–1930), creator of the most famous detective in history, Sherlock Holmes, came to London in 1891.

That same year he set up his eye treatment practice at 2 Upper Wimpole Street in nearby Marylebone and took up lodgings at 23 Montague Place for four months (long demolished and now part of Senate House Library).

'When I first came up to London I had rooms in Montague Street, just round the corner from The British Museum, and there I waited, filling in my too abundant leisure time by studying all those branches of science which might make me more efficient.' (*Memoirs of Sherlock Holmes* – 'The Adventure of the Musgrave Ritual', first published in *The Strand Magazine* in May 1893).

Architect Charles Forster Hayward (1830–1905) once lived at 20 Montague Street. The inventor and artist, John Oldham (1779–1840), who had invented a machine in 1809 to individually number banknotes, died at his home here.

Further down towards Great Russell Street, tucked away behind a tall, ivy-clad wall, is the Bedford Estates offices at No. 29a. The Bedford Estates offices link to the magnificent Bloomsbury House that extends around the corner to Great Russell Street. It was once occupied by architect Thomas Henry Wyatt (1807–80) who lived and died at the house. Bloomsbury House is currently occupied by the publishing house Faber & Faber Ltd and Faber Music Ltd.

Bloomsbury House, Montague Street side

The Bloomsbury Hotel – Great Russell Street

Simply called The Bloomsbury, this smart hotel is an elegantly restored neo-Georgian Grade II listed building. The hotel was designed by English architect Sir Edwin Lutyens (1869–1944) in 1928 and was extensively renovated in 2017. Situated opposite the Cheshire Hotel this swish building has a stylish entrance that is a photographer's treat. Next to this hotel, in total juxtaposition is the Trades Union Congress headquarters.

The Bloomsbury Street and Kenilworth Hotels

The Bloomsbury Street Hotel (left) and Kenilworth Hotel (right)

Looking west down Great Russell Street from The British Museum one notices two large hotels with domed turrets facing each other separated by Great Russell Street. To the left is The Radisson Blu Edwardian, Bloomsbury Street Hotel and, opposite, is The Radisson Blu Edwardian, Kenilworth Hotel: welcome to the Robert Cranston (1815–92) hotel empire. The Kenilworth Hotel was built first and was designed by George Waymouth (1825–1923) in 1903 followed by the Ivanhoe Hotel (now The Bloomsbury Street Hotel) by Sir Thomas Duncan Rhind (1871–1927) in 1906.

Helene Hanff (1916–97), the author of *84 Charing Cross Road* (1970), stayed at the Kenilworth Hotel when the British edition of the book was published in 1971. During her stay at the Kenilworth she came across, to some, as highly strung, which led to staff at the hotel awarding her the nickname the Duchess of Bloomsbury Street – the title she chose for her next book.

The Ivanhoe's Spy and Squatters (The Bloomsbury Street Hotel)

Inside this lavish hotel one will find contemporary décor, an original wrought-iron staircase and a display of pages from Virginia Woolf's, *Mrs Dalloway*. Chill-out dance music fills the dimly lit and stylish bar and restaurant; however, this hotel has a few modest stories to tell that I would like to share with you.

The Home Front Squatters of 1946

Home Front squatters

In 1946, London saw a wave of squatter's demonstrations, highlighting the lack of housing for both civilians and returning servicemen. During World War Two the Ivanhoe Hotel had been occupied by Irish labourers, employed to repair bomb-damaged buildings in the area. In 1946, twelve homeless families broke into the Ivanhoe Hotel. The on-looking crowd threw food parcels up to the squatters in sympathy. The Communist Party had been accused of helping to plan this and other demonstrations, and some members were eventually arrested. It was reported that people from the crowd shouted, 'is this what we won the war for?' The siege only lasted ten days after which the squatters left voluntarily and were housed temporarily in shelters before being finally rehoused.

Spy Arrested – 1965

British Secret Intelligence Service agent Frank Clifton Bossard (1912–2001) provided classified documents to the Soviet Union in the 1960s. In 1956, Bossard worked at the British Embassy in Bonn, West Germany, for the Secret Intelligence Service (MI6), his job was to interview and screen scientists and engineers who had left the Soviet Union. Bossard returned to London in 1961 to work for the Ministry of Aviation. Soviet agents realised that he had access to secret documents on guided missiles and, conveniently, a cash flow problem brought about by his lavish lifestyle needs.

In 1961, Bossard met a man called 'Gordon' in a local bar who revealed himself to be a Soviet agent. Gordon gave Bossard an advance of £250 to become a spy. Bossard was to listen to Radio Moscow for his coded instructions. Bossard took classified documents containing top secret information about missile and military electronic equipment from his office and photographed them in his hotel room during his lunch breaks. He was paid £2,000 for each packet of photographs delivered.

Bossard's newfound wealth and spending binges caught the attention of MI5 and he was arrested in 1965 at the Ivanhoe Hotel, the very place he had been photographing this secret content.

Bossard was sentenced to twenty-one years in prison at the Old Bailey in 1965, however, he was released early in 1975 and changed his name to Frank Russell Clifton. He gained employment with a firm of solicitors in Hull and married a Quaker where he lived a respectable life until he died in 2001.

A New Lease of Life for the Hotel

By 1976, Cranston's Ivanhoe Hotel went into liquidation and became The Radisson Edwardian, Marlborough Hotel. In 2008, the building received a massive £25 million refurbishment and the following year was renamed The Radisson Blu Edwardian, Bloomsbury Street Hotel. Today, with all its mod-cons and designer comfort the hotel still retains its former grand character.

The Museum Tavern

The Museum Tavern

Situated opposite The British Museum on the corner of Great Russell Street and Museum Street sits this historic tavern. Despite being in a busy and congested spot, the tavern somehow manages to offer seating al fresco. Inside this often very crowded pub one cannot help but admire the mahogany bar and ornate décor. The tavern offers real ales on tap and traditional food.

In 1723, this establishment opened as the Dog and Duck, representing the area's more rural times. Upon the opening of The British Museum, the owners changed the name to The British Museum Tavern in 1762. Later after refurbishment by William Finch Hill in 1858, who was a well-known music hall architect, the public house became the Museum Tavern. With its prime position, the tavern attracted locals such as Karl Marx, playwright J. B. Priestley, Sir Arthur Conan Doyle and George Orwell along with many more famous and influential punters.

Souvenir Press (Independent Book Publisher and Seller)

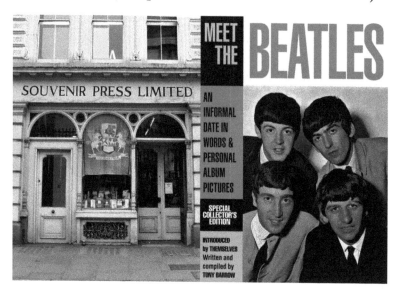

Souvenir Press bookshop (left). *Meet the Beatles* published by Souvenir Press (right)

One could be forgiven for walking straight passed this inconspicuous book publisher that is situated on the corner of Great Russell Street and Coptic Street.

Czech born Ernest Hecht (1929–2018) came to Britain as a Kindertransport child in 1939. Kindertransport (German for children's transport) rescued predominantly Jewish children and transported them to safer countries prior to the outbreak of the Second World War. Hecht read economics and commerce at The University of Hull and by 1951, and with just £250, started the Souvenir Press company. It is said that Souvenir Press was the first to publish rock'n'roll books in the UK, early publications include: *Tommy Steele* by John Kennedy (1958), *It's Great to be Young* by Cliff Richard (1960), and *Meet the Beatles* by the Beatles which was first published in 1963 and which is still in print today! Hecht believed that, 'publishers have the freedom and a duty to publish books of a minority interest, that they must invest in titles that are ahead of their time and that there are no rules in publishing'. He was a keen Arsenal and Brazil football fan and also produced concerts and presented theatrical productions. In 2003, The Ernest Hecht Charitable Foundation was set up to support the work of UK registered charities.

Ernest Hecht was a respected and popular member of the UK publishing industry. In 2001, he was awarded the first lifetime achievement award at the British Book Awards and received an OBE (Officer of the Order of the British Empire) in 2015. The Souvenir Press is one of the few remaining independently-owned major publishing houses in Britain and boasts around 500 titles. They specialise in non-fiction although they do have a wide variety of fiction available. The eclectic range of publications are truly absorbing, from parenting to science and the paranormal. Profile Books took over the publishing operations of Souvenir Press in 2018 and have maintained their name and unique character. The shop is (with the greatest of respect) 'a working shop': there is stuff everywhere, new and second-hand books are piled up on tables and squeezed horizontally and vertically into shelves. This quaint and slightly old-fashioned shop is a delightful reminder of what book hunting is all about. This inconspicuous and modest establishment has a lot to shout about.

Coincraft

Situated directly opposite The British Museum, this enchanting family business was established in 1955. Coincraft have been here since 1976 and have built up a highly respected and reputable business. The interior displays are reminiscent of the museum opposite with a tantalising collection of antiquities for sale that, in my non-expert opinion, are reasonably priced.

Inside this small, dark and quaint shop one discovers an intriguing variety of ancient and more recent coins, banknotes, medallions and antiquities. Amongst their antiquities are: Roman pottery; Egyptian artefacts; Saxon, Viking and Norman jewellery. The owners are more than happy for one to just browse and admire their treasure trove.

Jarndyce (Antiquarian Booksellers)

Inside Jarndyce bookshop

Situated next door to Coincraft, 46 Great Russell Street has been a bookseller since at least 1890.

The illustrator Randolph Caldecott lodged here between 1872 and 1879. Caldecott was known for his children's book illustrations, novels and foreign travel, humorous drawings of hunting and trends of the time. He produced cartoons and sketches of Parliament and sculptures, oil and watercolour paintings.

From around 1890, the firm of Luzac & Co (founded in Holland in the early 1700s) was the first company to use the building, and published and sold books specialising in the Middle and Far East until 1986.

Jarndyce Antiquarian Booksellers was established in 1969 in Covent Garden. In 1986, Jarndyce purchased No. 46 and the shop was renovated, restoring the interior to a nineteenth-century bookshop, an ideal setting to display eighteenth- and nineteenth-century books. Jarndyce publish up to eight catalogues a year covering a wide variety of subjects that include: Dickens; seventeenth- and eighteenth-century books and pamphlets, books in translation, Bloods and Penny Dreadfuls, Yellowback novels, plays and theatre, and newspapers.

The friendly staff will help one find what one wants regardless of one's budget. The shop is full of old-fashioned charm and has, apparently, a resident ghost or two that are not for sale!

South of Great Russell Street

Crossing over Great Russell Street the pace slows down as one leaves the hordes of tourists behind to explore the narrow streets with their small shops at this southern edge of Bloomsbury.

The Atlantis Bookshop (Modern Witchcraft) – Museum Street

As one walks along Museum Street, just before Bloomsbury Way, one will come across a small, pale blue shop. This is London's oldest independent occult bookshop and offers one an opportunity to discover modern witchcraft. The Atlantis Bookshop (Atlantis) has been a family-run bookshop since 1922. Mother and daughter, Bali and Geraldine Beskin currently run the shop. This intriguing and friendly shop sells everything from new and second-hand books including an excellent rare antiquarian section. Items also include: obsidian mirrors, candles and incense, a collection of silver jewellery, bags and clothes, magazines and a range of statues accommodating all spiritual tastes and traditions. Atlantis sells tarot cards and offers tarot readings (by appointment), and regularly holds events and meetings relating to the occult. The publishing section of Atlantis is Neptune Press who have published many books relating to the occult.

Wicca is mainly a western movement who practise witchcraft and nature worship. The religion is based on pre-Christian traditions. Gerald Brosseau Gardner (1884–1964), considered the father of modern Wicca, wrote a book in 1954 entitled *Witchcraft Today* and was the first book about witchcraft written by a self-proclaimed witch. Gardner founded Gardnerian Wicca, one of the leading traditions in the Wicca movement that became increasingly popular by the 1960s. Gardner held regular meetings in the basement of The Atlantis Bookshop.

Pied Bull Yard

Located more or less opposite The British Museum on the east side of Great Russell Street in Bury Place is Pied Bull Yard. This small courtyard contains some shops including London Review Bookshop, a Parisian-style Café Le Cordon Bleu and Truckles, a cosmopolitan modern wine bar and café.

The name of Pied Bull Yard can only be traced back to 1827. *John Rocque's map of London, 1746* names it as Stable Yard. There was a Pied Bull coaching inn on Museum Street and a Pied Bull tavern on Little Russell Street, leading one to believe that the yard catered for traders and shoppers at the Bloomsbury street market; however, no record of this has ever been found. The 1841 census lists the occupants of the yard as: coachman, coach maker, upholsterer, dressmaker and a livery keeper. This would suggest more of a mews arrangement at that time. Another belief is that, as the name suggests, it was a slaughter yard, which makes perfect sense to me. In 1940, during the London Blitz it is recorded by the *Bomb Site project* that a bomb fell close to Pied Bull Yard, which would explain the relatively modern yard that exists today.

The London Review Bookshop

The bookshop's forest green painted façade with gold signage and large windows, instantly depicts quality. This spacious and relatively new shop has become well established amongst London's cultural scene. The shop is located in Bury Place but can also be accessed from Pied Bull Yard.

The *London Review of Books* (*Review*) – a magazine of books that publishes twice a month – opened The London Review Bookshop with Alan Bennett cutting the ribbon in 2003. This acclaimed independent bookshop is a highly popular meeting place where one can talk, browse and eat cake! The shop holds a selection of more than 20,000 titles from world literature to contemporary fiction and poetry as well as every other genre one can imagine. One could easily lose track of time here.

The distinctive ethos of the *Review* –'intelligent without being pompous; engaged without being partisan' – is the key to their success. The shop is extremely popular with many authors and the public. The London Review Bookshop holds regular reader events with speakers that have included: Melvyn Bragg, Alan Bennett, Timothy Garton Ash and Alastair Campbell.

The attraction for me is simply the vast variety of good books and the friendly welcoming atmosphere. The bookshop has a wonderful cake shop that offers some exciting menus.

St George's Bloomsbury – Bloomsbury Way

St George's Bloomsbury

Set back and sandwiched into its confined space retreating from the busy Bloomsbury Way traffic, sits this delightful church with its neoclassical portico and unusual stepped tower looming above.

The flamboyant St George's is a Church of England parish church well known for its friendly welcome to visitors. They are pleased to welcome curious visitors who come to admire the church's eccentric architecture with its classical references and a bit of baroque thrown in for good measure!

During the mid-seventeenth and early part of the eighteenth century, new churches and homes were needed all over the city. London had had a terrible run of bad luck with the Great Plague in 1665 which was quickly proceeded by The Great Fire of London the following year. Many people from central London had lost their homes and businesses and migrated further out to places like Bloomsbury. This helped fuel rapid development around the Bloomsbury area.

In 1710, the Tories came to power and a year later passed the Fifty New Churches Act of 1711 which was funded by a coal tax. The Act intended to build churches in the new residential developments to relieve the overcrowded medieval parishes, however, only twelve churches were completed. The Commissioners for the Act led by architect Sir Christopher Wren (1632–1723) gave Bloomsbury their own parish church, St George's. Nicholas Hawksmoor (1662–1736) designed the church that was consecrated in 1730 by Edmund Gibson, Bishop of London and completed in 1731.

St George's, Bloomsbury is Hawksmoor's most distinctive work and features a statue of King George I in Roman dress at the top of a stepped pyramid-style spire, with statues of fighting lions and unicorns at the spire's base symbolising the end of the First Jacobite rising of 1715. The portico is based on the Roman Temple of Bacchus in Baalbek, Lebanon.

Spire of St George's Bloomsbury

Born in Russell Square, novelist Anthony Trollope (1815–82) was baptised at St George's. Emily Davison (1872–1913), the suffragette, who died at the Epsom Derby when she unexpectedly ran out on to the race course and was hit by the horse of King George V in 1913, had her memorial service at this church.

By the end of the twentieth century, the church was in urgent need of refurbishment and was restored back to its former glory by 2009. St George's is now a vibrant place of worship with a growing congregation. The inside is light and beautiful with a magnificent seventeenth-century Dutch chandelier loaned from the Victoria and Albert Museum. The church accommodates activities and events that include: adult education, lectures, social meetings, performances and concerts.

Museum of Comedy (Down in the Crypt)

If the tower and spire aren't controversial enough, below, steps lead one down to the crypt and welcome one into the wonderful world of comedy. The museum was founded by Leicester Square Theatre Director Martin Witts and was opened in 2014. The museum is dedicated to British comedy with a collection of memorabilia that includes: iconic props, photographs and posters, clothing and costumes, scripts, films and videos of British comedic performances. Artefacts range from: the much loved classic sitcom *Steptoe and Son*'s stuffed bear; the satirical puppet show *Spitting Image*'s puppet heads; to the legendary comedian and magician, Tommy Cooper's handmade magic props. There is also a small and intimate performance space (The Cooper Room) where one can see some top-class acts. The museum has established a good reputation in the world of comedy with big name acts performing to small audiences. This trip down memory lane is a reminder of how funny the British are and one should go in just for a laugh!

WEST

Fitzroy Square

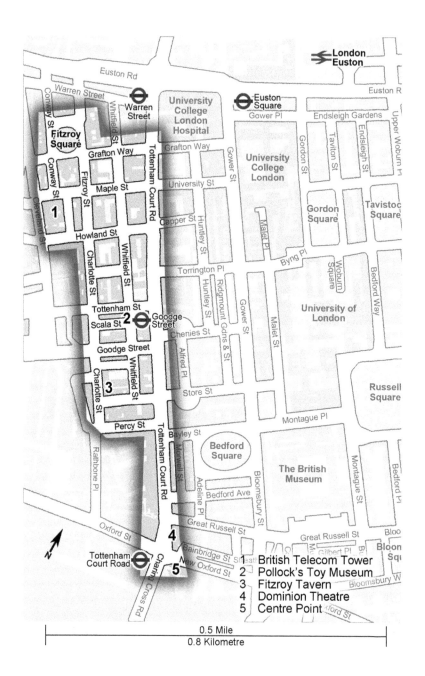

Euston Rd

London Euston

Warren Street

Warren Street

Conway St

Whitfield St

Euston Road

University College London Hospital

Euston Square

Gower Pl

Endsleigh Gardens

Upper Woburn Pl

Endsleigh St

Fitzroy Square

Grafton Way

Tottenham Court Rd

Grafton Way

Gower St

University College London

Gordon St

Taviton St

Conway St

Maple St

Fitzroy St

University St

Capper St

Huntley St

Gordon Square

Tavistock Square

1

Howland St

Maple St

Mallet Pl

Byng Pl

Woburn Square

Bedford Way

Whitfield St

Charlotte St

Torrington Pl

Huntley St

Ridgmount Gdns & St

Gower St

University of London

Mallet St

Bedford Way

Tottenham St

Goodge Street

2

Scala St

Chenies St

Alfred Pl

Goodge Street

Whitfield St

3

Charlotte St

Store St

Russell Square

Montague Pl

Percy St

Tottenham Court Rd

Bayley St

Maxwell St

Bedford Square

The British Museum

Montague St

Bedford Pl

Rathbone Pl

Adeline Pl

Bedford Ave

Bloomsbury St

4

Bedford Ave

Oxford St

Great Russell St

Great Russell St

Bloo

Tottenham Court Road

Charing Cross Rd

Bainbridge St

New Oxford St

Gilbert Pl

Bloom Squ

5

Bloomsbury W

1 British Telecom Tower
2 Pollock's Toy Museum
3 Fitzroy Tavern
4 Dominion Theatre
5 Centre Point

N

0.5 Mile
0.8 Kilometre

Welcome to the eastern part of the Fitzrovia neighbourhood that technically borders along Gower Street; however, once one has crossed Tottenham Court Road, the quirky Fitzrovian atmosphere takes over. Right on the doorstep of the West End, with its cosy streets, stylish shops and beautiful Fitzroy Square, this is certainly an area of contrasts.

Fitzrovia Mural by Simon Barber and Mick Jones
in Whitfield Gardens, Tottenham Court Road

Tottenham Court Road

Within the eastern part of Fitzrovia, this main artery starts at Euston Road and ends at Charing Cross Road where Oxford Street and New Oxford Street meet. Tottenham Court Road is west of Great Russell Street and is lined with department stores, electrical shops and everything else one would expect from a busy retail road. At its southern end, swarms of people pour out of Tottenham Court Road tube station in all directions to shop, work or be entertained in the West End.

Dominion Theatre

Dominion Theatre

Almost opposite Tottenham Court Road tube station with the Centre Point building towering overhead, the art deco Dominion Theatre (Dominion) stands wedged between two larger buildings. The theatre is a Grade II listed building and was designed by the architects William and T. R. Millburn.

***

The main part of the Dominion stands on the site of a former brewery, Meux's Horse Shoe Brewery that began its life in 1809 and was demolished in 1922. In 1814, one of the brewery's large beer vats burst, causing others to erupt, and emptying over a million litres of hot fermenting beer. The tide of beer crashed through the walls and rushed down Tottenham Court Road and the surrounding area, taking with it some slum houses and nine lives (the ninth person died a few days later from alcohol poisoning). The brewery was taken to court and found not guilty of negligence and the incident was written off as an Act of God.

***

The Dominion also occupies the site of the Court Cinema that opened in 1911 and closed in 1928. O'Brien's Fun Fair operated on this site for a short time and later in 1925, Luna Park, which was mainly a large tent hosting variety performances.

In 1929, the Dominion opened with its first show, a musical comedy called *Follow Through* that ran for only 148 performances and was followed by other unsuccessful shows. The Dominion failed as a live theatre and a year later was converted into a cinema and in 1933 was sold to Gaumont British. The theatre occasionally hosted concerts in the 1950s and 1960s, but its main use was as a cinema (in 1977 the preview of *Star Wars* was screened here).

By 1981, the Dominion was converted back to a live theatre. In 1993, the long-running musical *Grease* opened here, running for three years, (eventually moving to the Cambridge Theatre in 1996). Other significant performances staged at the theatre include: Disney's

Beauty and the Beast (1997–99), *Notre Dame de Paris* (2000–01) and a number of Royal Variety Performances (1992–2001).

One of the most popular West End musicals was staged here in 2002; based on the rock band Queen – Ben Elton's *We Will Rock You* – opened at the Dominion and ended 4,600 performances later in 2014. *We Will Rock You* is the longest-running show ever at the Dominion. Since then the theatre has had a major refurbishment restoring many of the original features, and is now a busy full-house theatre which welcomes one to the northern part of the West End. In 2018, Jim Steinman's *Bat Out of Hell – The Musical* arrived at the Dominion Theatre.

Centre Point – New Oxford Street

Centre Point

The brutalist yet slender architecture of the Centre Point tower is an iconic landmark, overlooking Bloomsbury and the West End. The tower is situated almost next door to the Dominion Theatre on New Oxford Street opposite Tottenham Court Road Station and less than a minute's walk from the west side of Great Russell Street. Don't worry, one will find it, just look up.

Property tycoon Harry Hyams gained planning permission in 1959 for the construction of Centre Point. Hyams owned the land that he then sold to London County Council (LCC) in exchange for liberal planning consent. This deal enabled the LCC to use part of this land to widen Tottenham Court Road; the LCC originally had plans to build a roundabout here. He signed a contract with the council to rent the site for 150 years at a rent of £18,500 per year.

A higher than normally permitted building was granted to Hyams and construction started in 1963. The 34-floor, 117 metre tall building was designed by Richard Seifert and Partners. It was completed by Wimpey Construction in 1966.

Hyams had Centre Point built with the intention that the entire tower would be occupied by a single tenant. He failed to find his single tenant and for many years, the building became known as London's Empty Skyscraper and was perceived as a symbol of greed. In 1974, student campaigners took a short occupation of the empty building, protesting on behalf of the homeless. They called the building 'a symbol of what was wrong with the property development business'.

By 1980, the building was occupied and became the headquarters of the Confederation of British Industry (CBI) until 2014. In 1995, Centre Point was awarded Grade II listed architectural status and was described as, 'one of the most distinctive high-rise compositions of the 1960s and a major London landmark'. Later in 2005, after being acquired by Targetfollow, a commercial property firm, Centre Point received a major refurbishment and remodelling.

In 2011, the building was acquired by Almacantar, a property investment and development company, and by 2015 work began on the total transformation of Centre Point. Almacantar commissioned Rick Mather Architects and Conran and Partners to convert eighty-two spaces into luxury apartments. The penthouse, at the time of writing this book, went on the market for around £55 million. A new square with shops and restaurants was built underneath the apartments. Alongside Centre Point is Crossrail's Tottenham Court Road station.

British Telecom Tower – Cleveland Street

British Telecom Tower

Standing in northern Fitzrovia and visible from across London, this iconic, slender, circular communication tower is a symbol of 1960s technology and optimism. When it was opened as Post Office Tower in 1964 it was declared an official secret due to its involvement in military communications. Photographs were forbidden and London's tallest tower did not appear on any Ordnance Survey maps until 1993 when this strange rule was lifted. This once secret tower was listed as a Grade II building in 2003.

Prime Minister Harold Wilson officially opened the tower in 1965. The main purpose of the tower was to support microwave aerials used to carry telecommunications traffic from London to the rest of the country. The architects were Eric Bedford and G. R. Yeats. Excluding the aerial rigging, the tower has a total height of 177 m (581 ft). In its heyday, the tower was famous for its revolving restaurant that offered spectacular views across London. The restaurant was opened to the public in 1966 by politician Tony Benn (1925–2014), then Postmaster General. Billy Butlin (1899–1980), the famous holiday camp entrepreneur, leased the restaurant known as the 'topofthetower', from 1966 until it closed in 1980. When it was first built the tower was the tallest building in London offering the public outstanding views across the capital, however, today it is not normally open to the general public. The tower remained London's tallest building until it lost its title to the 183 metre (600 feet) high Tower 42 built in the City of London in 1980.

View from the top of British Telecom Tower

Fitzroy Square and Garden

Fitzroy Square and Garden

Towards the north end of Fitzroy Street accompanied by the contrasting architecture of the British Telecom Tower looming overhead, is a smart, dignified and relaxing square and garden. Uniformed aristocratic houses grace the perimeter and look onto the square's enclosed garden. Around the well-kept and spacious square are partly pedestrianised areas with seating where one can relax and take in the sophisticated atmosphere and sense its rich past. The residents of Fitzroy Square are the proud key holders of the garden that is mainly closed to the public except for events such as the Open Garden Squares Weekend.

The Fitzroy family developed the area from the late eighteenth and early nineteenth century. Fitzroy Square provided residences for aristocratic families and was built in four stages. The eastern and southern sides were designed by Robert Adam and completed in 1798 by Adam's brothers James and William. The houses were fronted in Portland stone from the Isle of Portland in Dorset.

Due to a building slump during the Napoleonic Wars, construction of the square halted leaving the residents looking onto vacant ground. The northern and western sides, known for their stucco-fronted finish, were eventually built between 1827 and 1835. During World War Two, the south side was damaged by bombing and was rebuilt in the traditional style, in keeping with its surroundings.

Home of Virginia and Adrian Stephen from 1907 to 1911

***

Fitzroy Square has a generous proportion of blue plaques celebrating a wide range of important residents: Robert Gascoyne-Cecil, 3rd Marquess of Salisbury (1830–1903), who served as Prime Minister for three terms from 1885 for almost fourteen years, occupied No. 21. Bernard Shaw lived at No. 29 from 1887 to 1898 followed later by Virginia Woolf, known then as Virginia Stephen, who lived here with her brother Adrian from 1907 to 1911. In 1913, Roger Fry established the famous Omega Workshop and Studio at No. 33 until 1919.

Charlotte Street

Charlotte Street and Goodge Street

On first approach, Charlotte Street appears quite humble and modest; however, one soon realises its lively and cosmopolitan personality offers a mix of restaurants, nightlife and trendy designer shops. This was the home of Saatchi & Saatchi (world-renowned advertising agency) who occupied No. 80 from 1975 until vacating the tired building in 2016. Now demolished, a stylish new mixed-use building is under construction that is scheduled to open around 2020. With offices located at the northern end, many local residents still live above the colourful variety of retail businesses in the southern part.

Charlotte Street was named after Queen Charlotte (1744–1818), and before the Second World War was nicknamed Charlottenstrasse, after the German community who were living in the area. The street runs from Howland Street to Percy Street and is more or less in the centre of Fitzrovia. Charlotte Street was a centre for artists during the eighteenth century and is now a popular tourist attraction. The stylish Charlotte Street Hotel at the south end of the street is worth popping into for afternoon tea or cocktails.

The Fitzroy Tavern

The Fitzroy Tavern

As one approaches the brown and grey stone clad exterior of the tavern from Charlotte Street, one will notice two wrought-iron pub signs above. A mosaic tiled threshold with the words Fitzroy Tavern, embedded into it, welcomes one through the mahogany doors and into its dark, cosy interior. The tavern inside has been restored to its original Victorian glory and has snugs divided by glazed mahogany partitions. The ornate mahogany bars are a work of art in their own right and enhance the tavern's rustic charm. The walls are adorned with photographs and press cuttings of its historic past. Apart from the steady stream of tourists, one feels at home in a real London boozer!

The tavern originally opened as the Fitzroy Coffee House in 1883, and was later converted into a pub called The Hundred Marks in 1887 (believed to be due to the large number of Germans living in the area). The Hundred Marks was taken over by Russian tailor Judah Morris Kleinfeld in 1919 who rebranded it the Fitzroy Tavern. Eventually the licence passed to his daughter, Annie and her husband Charles Allchild, who ran the tavern into the 1950s. Their daughter Sally worked behind the bar from a very young age and later wrote a book about the pub, telling the story of its fascinating bohemian past. I would thoroughly recommend Sally Fiber's book, *The Fitzroy: The Autobiography of a London Tavern* (Sally died at eighty-one in 2017).

Between the 1920s and the mid-1950s the tavern became a famous meeting place for many of London's artists, intellectuals and the Bloomsbury Group. It was here that the Pennies from Heaven charity started, after the landlord witnessed a customer throwing a dart into the ceiling after losing a game. Kleinfeld decided that next time a customer wanted to throw darts at the ceiling, the darts would have money attached.

Fitzrovia is still proud of its down-to-earth pub culture where both the Bloomsbury and Fitzrovia worlds crossed over and happily coexisted. It is widely believed the modern name Fitzrovia originated from the Fitzroy Tavern. The name Fitzrovia first appeared in an article written for the 'William Hickey' social column of the *Daily Express* in 1940 by politician and writer Tom Driberg. In his article, he described his local pub the Fitzroy Tavern and its boozy bohemian regulars as Fitzrovians. It is, also, argued that Sri Lankan Tamil poet Meary James Tambimuttu first named the area Fitzrovia around 1938 to 1940 and apparently was, again, inspired by the Fitzroy Tavern.

***

Bohemians and entertainers who have frequented the establishment include: Jacob Epstein, Augustus John, Dylan Thomas and George Orwell. The comedians Kenneth Williams and Tommy Cooper were also regulars here. The tavern is currently owned by the Samuel Smith Brewery and remains popular with locals and visitors alike.

'*If you haven't visited the Fitzroy you haven't visited London.*'

Augustus John, 1927.

Pollock's Toy Museum – Scala Street

Pollock's Toy Museum

On the corner of Scala Street and Whitfield Street is Pollock's Toy Museum; one cannot miss it, understandably it is quite childish-looking! For some of us, the museum is a trip down memory lane. Benjamin Pollock was originally a toy theatre printer based in Hoxton (London) in the 1850s. The museum was created in 1956 by Marguerite Fawdry at Monmouth Street, near Covent Garden and soon became a success. In 1969, the museum moved to Scala Street.

The museum occupies two townhouses, one built in the 1780s and the other one hundred years later. The floorboards creak with age as one enters the museum's small rooms which are packed with Victorian toys, dolls, teddy bears and toys from around the world. The rooms also display dolls' houses and puppets, not to mention some magnificent toy theatres. It also has its own small toyshop full of good old-fashioned tactile playthings.

The Hope Fitzrovia – Tottenham Street

Next door to the toy museum, the big kids can enjoy a pint or two. The dark battleship grey exterior of this public house does not easily give away its age. It has been serving punters since 1809, and today one can tuck into a traditional pie washed down with a pint of ale.

Cheers!

BIBLIOGRAPHY

Ackroyd, Peter. *London: the Biography*. Chatto & Windus, 2000.

Bakewell, Michael. *Fitzrovia: London's Bohemia*. National Portrait Gallery, 1999.

Barker, Felix, and Peter Jackson. *The History of London in Maps*. Barrie and Jenkins, 1992.

Boulter, Michael Charles. *Bloomsbury Scientists: Science and Art in the Wake of Darwin*. UCL Press, 2017.

Brooker, Peter. *Bohemia in London: the Social Scene of Early Modernism*. Palgrave Macmillan, 2004.

Byrne, Andrew. *Bedford Square: an Architectural Study*. The Athlone Press, 1990.

Dargan, Pat. *Georgian London: the West End*. Amberley, 2012.

Denford, Steven L. J., et al. *Streets of Bloomsbury: a Survey of Streets, Buildings & Former Residents in a Part of Camden*. Camden History Society, 2016.

Du Prey, Pierre de la Ruffinière. *Hawksmoor's London Churches: Architecture and Theology*. University of Chicago Press, 2002.

Elkin, Stephen L. *Politics and Land Use Planning: the London Experience*. Cambridge University Press, 2010.

Fiber, Sally, and Clive Powell-Williams. *The Fitzroy: the Autobiography of a London Tavern*. Sally Fiber/DeSapinaud, 2014.

Freitas, Ricci De. *From Fields to Fountains: the Story of Bloomsbury's Russell Square*. Marchmont Association, 2016.

Freitas, Ricci De. *The Story of Marchmont Street: Bloomsbury's Original High Street*. Marchmont Association, 2012.

Görner, Rüdiger. *London Fragments: a Literary Expedition*. Haus Pub./Armchair Traveller, 2010.

Hamilton, James. *The British Museum*. Head of Zeus, 2018.

Harte, N. B. *The University of London: 1836–1986: An Illustrated History*. Athlone Press, 1986.

Harte, N. B., and John A. North. *The World of UCL, 1828–2004*. UCL Press, 2004.

Hartley, Jenny. *Charles Dickens: an Introduction*. Oxford University Press, 2016.

Hawksley, Lucinda. *London Treasury*. Carlton Books Ltd, 2016.

Hayes, David A., and F. Peter. Woodford. *East of Bloomsbury*. Camden History Society, 1998.

Hibbert, Christopher, et al. *The London Encyclopaedia*. Macmillan, 2010.

Hudson, Roger. *Bloomsbury, Fitzrovia & Soho*. Haggerston Press, 1996.

Ingleby, Matthew. *Bloomsbury: Beyond the Establishment*. The British Library, 2018.

Inwood, Stephen. *A History of London*. Papermac, 2000.

Lee, Hermione. *Virginia Woolf: Hermione Lee*. Vintage, 1997.

Licence, Amy. *Living in Squares, Loving in Triangles: the Lives and Loves of Virginia Woolf and the Bloomsbury Group*. Amberley Publishing, 2016.

Melhuish, Clare, and F. Peter Woodford. *The Life & Times of the Brunswick, Bloomsbury*. Camden History Society, 2006.

Merrington, W. R. *University College Hospital and Its Medical School: a History*. Heinemann, 1976.

Millar, Stephen. *London's City Churches*. Metro Publications Ltd, 2005.

Murray, Nicholas. *Real Bloomsbury*. Seren, 2010.

Nash, Jay Robert. *Spies: a Narrative Encyclopedia of Dirty Deeds and Double Dealing from Biblical Times to Today*. Evans, 1997.

Porter, Roy. *London, a Social History*. Harvard University Press, 2001.

Pugh, Gillian. *London's Forgotten Children: Thomas Coram and the Foundling Hospital*. Tempus, 2007.

Rennison, Nick. *The Book of Lists: London*. Canongate, 2007.

Rosner, Victoria. *The Cambridge Companion to the Bloomsbury Group*. Cambridge University Press, 2014.

Service, Alastair, and W. J. Toomey. *The Architects of London and Their Buildings from 1066 to the Present Day*. Architectural Press, 1979.

Spalding, Frances. *The Bloomsbury Group*. National Portrait Gallery, 2013.

Stewart, Rachel. *The Town House in Georgian London*. Yale University Press, 2009.

Telfer, Kevin. *The Remarkable Story of Great Ormond Street Hospital*. Simon & Schuster, 2008.

Walford, Edward. *Old London: Hyde Park to Bloomsbury*. Village Press, 1989.

PICTURE CREDITS

Most of the following images are available under Creative Commons (CC) from Wikimedia Commons: https://commons. wikimedia.org (accessed 2018). Historical images not mentioned have no known copyright restrictions and all non-credited contemporary images are the copyright of the author.

A Brief Description of Bloomsbury
Bloomsbury Festival 2018: Agnese Sanvito. www.agnesesanvito. com, cropped from original.

Bloomsbury Group
Some of the members of the Bloomsbury Group (Bloomsbury.gif): Bernhard Wenzl (CC BY 3.0), adapted from original.

East
Foundling Hospital 1770: Wellcome Collection (CC BY 4.0), enhanced from original.

The Rugby Tavern: Ewan Munro (CC BY-SA 2.0), cropped and edited from original.

North Central (The university district)
Senate House Library, University of London: University of London.

London University, coloured engraving: University College, London: the main building. Coloured engraving: Wellcome Collection (CC BY 4.0), cropped and edited from original.

Jeremy Bentham's dressed skeleton: Philafrenzy (CC BY-SA 4.0), cropped and edited from original.

Mummified head: Jeremy Bentham's Severed Head: Ethan Doyle White (CC BY-SA 4.0), cropped and edited from original.

Senate House under construction: University of London.

George Orwell, 1940: Cassowary Colorizations (CC BY 2.0).

North London Hospital, Lithograph 1834: North London Hospital (renamed University College Hospital) façade, Lithograph, c. 1834. Courtesy of Wellcome Collection (CC BY 4.0), cropped and edited from original.

The old University College Hospital, now called Cruciform Building: Medical district picture Cruciform from air: Andro Loria Photography, London, UK. http://androloria.com, cropped from original.

North Central

Sir Henry Wellcome: Sir Henry Solomon Wellcome. Photograph by Lafayette Ltd: Wellcome Collection (CC BY 4.0), cropped and edited from original.

The Human Genome Bookcase, Wellcome Collection Medicine Now: Kerr/ Noble creator of the books, and Gitta Gschwendtner as the creator of the bookcase, Wellcome Collection, cropped from original.

Statuette of an Egyptian man and his wife, 18th Dynasty: The Petrie Museum of Egyptian Archaeology: Osama Shukir Muhammed Amin (CC BY-SA 4.0).

South Central

John Rocque's Map of London, 1746: courtesy of the David Rumsey Map Collection, www.davidrumsey.com, cropped and edited from original.

The British Museum in Montagu House: The British Museum in Montagu House the Russell Street façade coloured aquatint: Courtesy of Wellcome Collection (CC BY 4.0), cropped and enhanced from original.

Meet the Beatles (published by Souvenir Press): Courtesy of Souvenir Press Ltd, cropped from original.

Inside Jarndyce book shop: Ed Nassau Lake, Jarndyce, Antiquarian Booksellers, cropped from original.

Spire of St George's Bloomsbury: Tony Hisgett (CC BY 2.0).

West

Fitzrovia Mural by Simon Barber and Mick Jones in Whitfield Gardens, on Tottenham Court Road: Wall: Tony Hisgett (CC BY 2.0), cropped from original.

View from the top of BT Tower: Howard Lake (CC BY-SA 2.0), Cropped, edited and enhanced from original.

Charlotte Street and Goodge Street: Philafrenzy (CC BY-SA 4.0).

Cheers! Rawpixel.com – Freepik.com.

All maps: © Edward Arnold: Base maps © maproom.net.

INDEX

Note: *italicised* page numbers denote illustrations, and **bold** ones denote tables.

Radisson Blu Edwardian Bloomsbury Street Hotel

Lightning Source UK Ltd.
Milton Keynes UK
UKHW020642070619
343990UK00006B/53/P